UNBEATABLE CHICKEN RECIPES

Lou Seibert Pappas

BRISTOL PUBLISHING ENTERPRISES
San Leandro, California

a nitty gritty® cookbook

Printed in the United States of America.

ISBN 1-55867-189-7

Cover design: Frank J. Paredes
Cover photography: John A. Benson
Food stylist: Susan Massey
Illustrator: James Balkovek

CONTENTS

CHICKEN: A WEALTH OF ASSETS

Beloved by all ages, chicken continues to escalate in popularity. It showcases a wealth of assets — it's healthful, economical, versatile, quick and easy to fix and convenient. Because chicken can be prepared in countless ethnic styles, it offers ongoing, lasting appeal for everyday and festive meals.

High in protein and low in saturated fat, chicken contributes many benefits to today's diet. Its skinless white meat is lower in calories and cholesterol than most red meats. Both the white and dark meat are rich in iron and B vitamins. Chicken is also prized for its good dollar value. Whole chickens are particularly economical. The cost of chicken per pound varies widely, ranging from low for whole birds to relatively high for boneless, skinless breast meat. You can save considerably by cutting up your own chicken.

One of the most versatile foods, chicken is ideal for quick snacks, everyday family meals and even festive guest occasions. Chicken parts are popular because they are so convenient, quick to prepare and ultra-versatile. Buying cut-up chicken parts lets you match purchases to dining preferences of light or dark meat. The breasts, in particular, cook swiftly. They can be prepared in innumerable global styles in just a few minutes. What a time-saver for busy households!

ABOUT CHICKEN

BUYING CHICKEN

It is important to buy chicken as fresh as possible, so shop at a busy market that has a quick turnover. Look for a high-breasted, plump bird with taut skin. The skin color can range from pure white to golden yellow, depending on the diet of, age of and processing method used for the bird. If you purchase packaged cut-up chicken, choose packages with little or no liquid in the bottom tray and avoid any packages with spots of blood.

TYPES OF CHICKEN

- **Cornish hens** are miniature chickens, about 5 to 6 weeks old, and weigh no more than 2 pounds.
- **Broilers**, also called **fryers**, account for about 90% of all chickens marketed in the United States. These typically weigh between 3 and 3½ pounds and are usually about 7 weeks old. Despite the name, broiler-fryers are an all-around bird, ideal for grilling or broiling, sautéing, stir-frying and roasting.
- **Roasters** are usually about 2½ months old and weigh 5 to 6 pounds or more, providing lots of meat per serving. They are perfect for a roasted chicken dinner.

- **Heavy hens**, or **stewing hens**, weigh in at $4\frac{1}{2}$ to 6 pounds and are considerably older and less tender than broiler-fryers and roasters. They are best used for long-simmered dishes such as soups and stews.

STORING AND HANDLING CHICKEN

Once purchased, leave chicken in the market's wrapping to avoid introducing bacteria into your kitchen and store it in the coldest part of the refrigerator. Plan to cook it or freeze it within 2 days. Well-wrapped whole chickens have a 1-year freezer life at 0°; frozen chicken parts should be used within 9 months. Be sure to label and date all packages.

The safest way to thaw frozen poultry is in the refrigerator. Allow about 12 to 24 hours for a whole bird, or 4 to 10 hours for parts; the time will vary with the size of the chicken or the number of parts in the package.

Today's factory-bred chickens are prone to contamination from salmonella bacteria, which can cause food poisoning. Fortunately, the cooking process kills most bacteria. Problems do arise when cross-contamination occurs, so be extra careful to avoid using tools and surfaces that have come in contact with raw chicken before cleaning them. Thoroughly wash tools and surfaces with hot soapy water after handling or cutting chicken. Wipe down wooden or plastic cutting boards with a diluted solution of bleach (about 1 tablespoon bleach to 1 quart water) and rinse well.

Once cooked, chicken leftovers should be refrigerated as soon as possible. Never let them stand at room temperature for more than 2 hours. Plan to consume cooked chicken within 2 to 3 days.

CUTTING A WHOLE CHICKEN INTO PARTS

It's relatively easy to cut a whole chicken into parts and is an economical pursuit. Place the chicken on a cutting board breast-side down. With a sharp knife, cut through the backbone along the spinal column. Flip the chicken over and, with the heel of your hand, push down on the breastbone to flatten the chicken. Remove the wings by cutting through the joint that attaches the wing to the breast; cut off the wing tips and save them for stock if desired. Grasp one leg and slice the skin where the thigh joins the body. Bend back the leg until the thigh joint pops up and cut around the thigh to remove the leg from the body. Repeat with the other leg. Separate the thighs from the drumsticks at the joint. Cut away the side of the breast separating it from the tiny bones and cut the whole breast in half.

The chicken is now in 8 pieces ready for cooking. The backbones, neck and innards can be used for stock or other uses. Freeze the liver separately, collecting a quantity to use in a paté or other dish at a later date.

Removing the skin from the chicken parts is simple. Wearing rubber gloves, hold the chicken part in one hand and peel back the skin with the other hand. When skinning the drumsticks, it helps to have a paper towel in the hand that you use to peel back the skin, to keep the hand from slipping. Discard the skin.

Chicken cutlets are breasts that have been skinned, boned and pounded evenly thin. They are ideal for many quick dishes. To make chicken cutlets, slide a sharp knife along the breastbone to cut the meat away from the bone; peel off the skin. Pound skinless, boneless breasts lightly with a round mallet between 2 sheets of plastic wrap or waxed paper until about 1/4-inch thick.

COOKING CHICKEN

Chicken can be prepared with any cooking method. Roasting, a dry heat process, is popular for a whole bird. Opinions vary on the correct oven temperature. Some favor a low constant temperature, around 350°. This method reduces shrinkage, yet the white meat can become dry. Some suggest roasting chickens at a high temperature to start, about 425° to 450°, and finishing at a lower temperature, around 350° to 375°. This method sears the bird and retains juices, yet the skin will not be crispy and the white meat can be slightly drier than the dark. However, this method is ideal to choose when you want to use the flavorful pan drippings for a sauce. The method of roasting chicken at a constant high temperature, 450° to 475°, has been applauded for producing both moist dark and white meat and a beautifully browned bird with taut skin. Its one drawback is that the pan juices can become too dark and dry to use for a sauce. To avoid overbrowning, chopped vegetables with about 1/4 cup water can be placed under the bird during roasting; they will enhance a flavorful sauce at the finish.

To avoid the risk of contamination, it is highly recommended that birds be roasted *unstuffed*, with the stuffing cooked in a separate pan. However, to add flavor to a chicken, herbs and seasonings can be tucked under the breast and thigh skin of a whole bird. Also, individual chicken breasts can be stuffed with a pesto or other seasoning before cooking.

Whether to truss a bird or not is a personal decision. Some pros claim that tying the legs together makes for more even cooking and a neater looking finished bird. I like the free-form open look of a bird roasted without trussing. However, tuck the wing tips under the back before roasting to prevent burning. Once roasted, it is important to let the bird sit for 10 to 15 minutes after removing it from the oven. This helps it to retain juices and relax its fibers, which results in more tender meat.

Besides roasting, broiling, grilling, poaching, sautéing and braising are all wonderful ways to cook whole chickens and their parts.

- Broiling is best suited to cooking small pieces of chicken, such as breasts, drumsticks and thighs.
- Grilling or barbecuing can be done with parts on an open grill, or with a whole chicken in a covered grill or on a rotisserie.
- Poaching is one of the simplest ways to cook a whole chicken and results in moist and tender meat as well as a flavorful stock that you can use for other dishes.
- Sautéing is a method of browning parts in a skillet with a small amount of fat in a short amount of time.
- Braising or stewing is a slow method of cooking with moist heat in a heavy pan, either on the stovetop or in the oven.

TESTING CHICKEN FOR DONENESS

To test for doneness when roasting a whole bird, an instant-read thermometer provides a handy, accurate gauge. Slip the tool into the thickest part of the breast, without touching the bone. It should read 170°. Without a thermometer, test for doneness by cutting a slit in the flesh between the leg and the body; if the juices run clear, the bird is done; pink juices indicate that more cooking is necessary. When testing chicken parts for doneness, insert a small knife and check to see if the juices run clear; if pink, more cooking is needed.

APPETIZERS AND SANDWICHES

PISTACHIO-STUDDED CHICKEN TERRINE

Servings: 10

Lively with spices and lemon zest, this green, pistachio-laden terrine makes a handsome picnic entrée or first course.

2 tsp. olive oil
1 large onion, finely chopped
4 boneless, skinless chicken breast
    halves
1 lb. lean ground pork
1 tsp. salt
1/2 tsp. dried thyme
1/2 tsp. ground allspice
1 tsp. grated fresh lemon peel (zest)
1/4 tsp. freshly ground pepper

1/4 tsp. nutmeg
1 egg
1 egg white
1/3 cup nonfat dry milk powder
1/3 cup chicken stock
2 tbs. dry sherry
2 cloves garlic, minced
6 tbs. pistachio nuts
2 bay leaves
6 black peppercorns

Heat oven to 325°. In a small skillet over medium heat, heat oil and sauté onion until soft. Grind chicken with a food processor or food grinder and place in a bowl with sautéed onion, pork, salt, thyme, allspice, lemon peel, pepper, nutmeg, egg, egg white, milk powder, stock, sherry and garlic. Mix until blended.

Spread half of the meat mixture in a greased 8-x-4½-inch loaf pan. Sprinkle with half of the nuts. Cover with remaining meat mixture and sprinkle with remaining nuts. Arrange bay leaves and peppercorns in a decorative manner over the top of terrine. Cover with aluminum foil. Place loaf pan in a roasting pan. Add water to roasting pan to come 1 inch up the sides of loaf pan. Bake for 1½ hours, or until cooked through. Remove loaf pan from water bath and refrigerate for 1 day before serving. To serve, unmold terrine and cut into ½-inch-thick slices.

CHICKEN, JICAMA AND MUSHROOM CREPES

The fresh crunch of jicama augments a chicken and mushroom filling, which plumps up these rolled crepes. For a light entrée, this recipe serves 4 to 5.

CREPES
2 eggs
¾ cup milk
½ cup all-purpose flour
¼ tsp. salt
butter

FILLING
4 boneless, skinless chicken breast halves
½ cup chicken stock
¼ cup dry white wine
2 tsp. chopped fresh tarragon, or
    ½ tsp. dried
salt and ground white pepper to taste
1 tbs. cornstarch blended with 1 tbs.
    cold water
½ lb. white mushrooms, sliced
2 shallots, chopped
1 tsp. olive oil
½ cup diced jicama
1 tsp. grated fresh lemon peel (zest)
¼ cup (1 oz.) freshly grated Parmesan
    or Romano cheese
chopped fresh chives for garnish

For crepes, place eggs, milk, flour and salt in a blender container or food processor workbowl and blend just until smooth. Let stand for at least 30 minutes and up to 1 hour. Heat a 6-inch crepe pan or skillet over medium heat and add ½ tsp. butter. When butter is melted, pour about 2 tbs. of the batter into pan, tilting pan to cover surface with batter. Cook for about 1 minute, or until crepe is browned underneath. Turn and cook opposite side. Remove crepe from pan and repeat with remaining batter. Stack crepes, cover with plastic wrap and refrigerate if made ahead.

For filling, place chicken in a large skillet and add chicken stock, wine, tarragon, salt and pepper. Bring to a boil, cover, reduce heat to low and simmer for 8 to 10 minutes, or until chicken is cooked through. Remove chicken, cool and dice. Bring cooking liquid to a boil and stir in cornstarch mixture. Cook, stirring, until thickened to a sauce consistency. In a large skillet over medium heat, sauté mushrooms and shallots in oil for about 2 minutes, until softened. Add jicama and lemon peel and cook for 1 minute. Mix in diced chicken, sauce and cheese.

Heat oven to 375°. Place a spoonful of filling down the center of 1 crepe and roll up cigar-fashion. Place in a greased 9-x-13-inch baking pan and repeat with remaining crepes and filling. Bake for about 10 minutes, or until crepes are hot throughout. Serve crepes on small plates garnished with chopped chives.

SPINACH-WRAPPED SESAME CHICKEN WITH TWO DIPPING SAUCES

For a tantalizing hors d'oeuvre with an inviting presentation, offer a choice of dipping sauces for chicken morsels cloaked in spinach wrappers.

½ cup chicken stock
2 tsp. low-sodium soy sauce
few drops sesame oil
3 chicken breast halves
1 bunch spinach

SESAME YOGURT DIP

¾ cup plain yogurt
1 tbs. toasted sesame seeds
¼ tsp. ground cumin
salt and freshly ground pepper to taste

CHUTNEY SAUCE

½ cup mango chutney
2 tbs. frozen orange juice concentrate, thawed
¼ cup low-fat sour cream

Place stock, soy sauce and sesame oil in a medium saucepan and heat until simmering. Add chicken breasts and simmer for about 10 minutes, or until just tender. Drain and reserve stock for another use if desired. Cool chicken and remove and discard skin and bones. Cut meat into chunks about ½-inch wide and 1-inch long. Cook spinach in boiling salted water for 30 seconds; drain. Rinse spinach under cold running water and drain again; remove and discard stems.

To assemble, wrap each piece of chicken in a spinach leaf and arrange on a platter. Stir together yogurt, sesame seeds, cumin, salt and pepper and spoon into a bowl. With a blender or food processor, blend chutney, orange juice concentrate and sour cream and spoon into a bowl. Provide a small container of toothpicks to skewer chicken and dip into sauces.

MUSHROOM AND CHICKEN TRIANGLES

Makes 48

Paper-thin filo dough encases these savory hot pastry triangles. Assemble in advance and refrigerate for several hours before baking, if you wish.

3 green onions, with half of the green
    tops, chopped
1 tsp. olive oil
¾ lb. white mushrooms, finely chopped
1 clove garlic, minced
2 cups shredded cooked chicken
1 egg
3 oz. ricotta cheese

¾ cup (3 oz.) shredded Gruyère or
    Jarlsberg cheese
3 tbs. chopped fresh flat-leaf parsley
½ cup soft French or Italian
    breadcrumbs
16 sheets filo dough
¼ cup butter, melted

Heat oven to 350°. In a large skillet over medium heat, sauté onions in oil until softened. Add mushrooms and garlic and sauté for about 2 minutes. In a bowl, mix together chicken, mushroom mixture, egg, cheeses, parsley and breadcrumbs. Lay filo on a work surface and cover with plastic wrap. Using 1 sheet at a time, brush filo with melted butter; cover with another sheet and brush with butter. Cut into six 3-inch-wide strips. Place a rounded teaspoonful of filling at one end of each strip. Fold each strip like a flag and place seam-side down on a greased baking sheet. Brush with butter. Repeat with remaining filo and filling. Bake for 15 minutes, or until golden brown.

SESAME CHICKEN WINGS

The wings make a tasty appetizer to nibble out of hand. Have damp paper towels handy for wiping fingers.

1 clove garlic, mashed
2 tbs. plain yogurt
2 tbs. Dijon mustard
8 chicken wings
3 tbs. fine dry sourdough breadcrumbs
1 tsp. sesame seeds
1 tbs. olive oil
salt and freshly ground pepper to taste

Heat broiler. In a bowl, stir together garlic, yogurt and 1 tbs. of the mustard. Cut off tips from chicken wings. Reserve for another use, such as for chicken stock, or discard. Add remaining wing portions to yogurt mixture and marinate for 10 minutes. Place wings on a broiling pan and broil for 5 minutes per side, turning once. In a small bowl, mix together breadcrumbs, sesame seeds, oil, salt and pepper. Spread wings with remaining mustard and dip in breadcrumb mixture. Broil until crisp and golden, about 2 minutes, turning once.

ARAM SANDWICHES WITH CHICKEN, TOMATOES AND BASIL

Armenian cracker bread, called lavosh, becomes flexible for rolling up into a cylinder after a bath under running water. Recently, lavosh has become available in a soft, pliable version as well. Filled with thinly sliced chicken breast and salad makings, it turns into a colorful pinwheel sandwich or appetizer. Use leftover roasted or barbecued chicken, thinly sliced, if desired.

1 large round lavosh
8 oz. soft light-style cream cheese
2 tsp. Dijon mustard
2 cooked boneless, skinless chicken breasts, thinly sliced
2 large tomatoes, sliced as thinly as possible
½ cup fresh basil leaves
about 6 outer leaves romaine lettuce, center ribs removed
chopped fresh chives for garnish

Dampen 1 large or 2 small kitchen towels and wring out excess moisture. Moisten crisp lavosh well on both sides under cold running water. Place lavosh, darker side down, between layers of damp towel and set aside until soft and pliable, about 45 minutes. Remove top towel. If using soft lavosh, omit this step and place darker side down on a work surface.

Mix cheese with mustard and spread evenly over lavosh. Cover with chicken. Top with tomatoes, basil and romaine, stopping about 4 inches from the far edge. Sprinkle with chives. Lift towel to fold the near edge of lavosh over filling about 1 inch. Roll up sandwich gently, but firmly, jelly roll-fashion. Wrap rolled sandwich with plastic wrap and chill for 1 to 24 hours.

When ready to serve, remove plastic wrap and cut into 3/4-inch slices.

GRILLED CHICKEN AND
CRANBERRY RELISH SANDWICHES

With a jar of fresh cranberry relish or chutney on hand, this makes a quick, scrumptious sandwich. If you have roasted or poached chicken available, use it instead of grilling the breasts. If desired, spread the toast with light sour cream or mayonnaise mixed with a little grated orange zest.

2 boneless, skinless chicken breast
    halves, slightly flattened to uniform
    thickness
2 tbs. olive oil
1/4 tsp. dried thyme
1/4 tsp. dried tarragon

salt and freshly ground pepper to taste
4 thick slices country bread
Dijon mustard
1/4 cup cranberry relish or chutney
alfalfa sprouts for garnish
butter or green leaf lettuce for garnish

Prepare a hot barbecue fire, or heat grill or broiler to high. Brush chicken with 1 tbs. of the olive oil and sprinkle with thyme, tarragon, salt and pepper. Grill or broil for about 4 minutes per side, or until cooked through. Brush bread with remaining oil and toast lightly on grill or under broiler; spread lightly with mustard.

To assemble, slice chicken on the diagonal and layer on 2 pieces of toasted bread. Top with relish and garnish with sprouts and lettuce. Top with remaining toasted bread.

GRILLED CHICKEN AND SUN-DRIED TOMATO PESTO SANDWICHES

This is a popular offering at a local bistro and wine bar, served paired with a choice of coleslaw or potato salad. In my version, I like to tuck fresh arugula from the garden into the sandwich alongside the chicken.

2 boneless, skinless chicken breast halves, slightly flattened to uniform thickness
2 tbs. olive oil
salt and freshly ground pepper to taste
1 tsp. chopped fresh oregano, or ¼ tsp. dried

1 tsp. chopped fresh tarragon, or ¼ tsp. dried
4 thick slices country bread
6 tbs. *Sun-Dried Tomato Pesto*, page 154
½ cup arugula leaves

Prepare a hot barbecue fire, or heat grill or broiler to high. Brush chicken with 1 tbs. of the olive oil and sprinkle with salt, pepper, oregano and tarragon. Grill or broil for about 3 to 4 minutes per side, or until cooked through. Brush bread with remaining oil and toast lightly on grill or under broiler; spread with pesto.

To assemble, slice chicken on the diagonal and layer on 2 pieces of toasted bread. Top with arugula and remaining toasted bread.

CHICKEN PITA POCKETS

Whole wheat pita breads make a cushiony, savory container for a chicken and feta salad medley.

4 whole wheat pita breads
3 cooked boneless, skinless chicken breast
    halves, or 4 cooked boneless, skinless
    chicken thighs, cut into strips
1/4 lb. feta or goat cheese, crumbled
1/4 lb. white mushrooms, sliced
12 cherry tomatoes, halved
1/2 cup shredded fresh basil leaves
2 green onions, chopped
1/3 cup plain yogurt
3 tbs. toasted pistachio nuts, pine nuts or sunflower kernels

Heat oven to 350°. Slit open one side of pita breads and wrap breads with aluminum foil. Bake for 10 minutes, or until heated through. Mix together chicken, cheese, mushrooms, tomatoes, basil, onions, yogurt and nuts. Stuff filling into warm pita pockets.

PLATE-SIZED CHICKEN TACOS

Makes 4

Soft tortillas enclose the typical Mexican sandwich and create a warm and inviting backdrop for chicken and black beans. This makes a quick impromptu supper with leftover cooked chicken on hand. It is especially fun to use plate-sized tortillas for a dramatic serving. Assemble all the ingredients ahead of time so that you are ready to make and serve the tacos at the same moment.

four 9-inch flour tortillas
1½ cups cooked, seasoned black
    beans, mashed slightly
1⅓ cups shredded cooked chicken
1 cup shredded green cabbage or
    iceberg lettuce

2 green onions, chopped
1 Roma tomato, diced
½ cup (2 oz.) crumbled queso ranchero
    cheese or mild feta cheese
taco sauce

In a large skillet over medium heat, heat tortillas, one at a time, for about 1 minute on one side; turn and heat the other side for about 30 seconds.

To assemble, place 1 tortilla on a plate, spread with ¼ of the beans and sprinkle with ¼ each of the chicken, cabbage, onions, tomato and cheese. Drizzle with taco sauce. Roll up cigar-fashion. Repeat with remaining tortillas.

SOUPS

POACHED CHICKEN
AND CHICKEN STOCK

Makes about 3 cups diced
chicken plus chicken stock

The moist juicy meat that comes from poaching a chicken has myriad uses in salads, soups, pizzas and pasta dishes. Vary the seasonings slightly by adding 2 star anise pods or several slices of slivered fresh ginger if the final dish has Asian overtones.

1 broiler-fryer, about 3-3½ lb.
cold water
1 small onion studded with 2 whole cloves
1 stalk celery, trimmed and cut into
    2-inch pieces

1 carrot, peeled and cut into 1-inch
    pieces
3 sprigs fresh parsley
salt to taste
6 peppercorns

Place chicken in a large saucepan and add cold water to cover chicken halfway. Add remaining ingredients and bring to a boil. Reduce heat, cover and simmer for about 50 minutes, or until chicken is cooked through. Cool chicken slightly in stock. Pour stock into a tall container and refrigerate. When cold, lift off congealed fat on the surface of stock and discard. Remove skin and bones from chicken meat. Discard skin and bones and reserve meat for another use. Keep stock and meat refrigerated for up to 3 days or freeze stock for longer storage.

AVGOLEMONO PISTACHIO SOUP

The Greek way of whisking lemon and eggs with chicken stock results in a remarkable low-calorie, yet filling, soup.

3 cups richly flavored low-fat chicken stock
1½ tbs. cornstarch
1½ tbs. cold water
3 eggs
¼ cup fresh lemon juice
lemon slices for garnish
2 tbs. chopped pistachio nuts for garnish

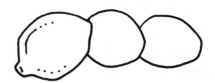

In a medium stockpot, heat chicken stock to boiling. Mix cornstarch and water to form a paste, stir into boiling stock and cook for 2 minutes. In a large bowl, whisk together eggs and lemon juice and pour ½ of the stock into egg mixture, whisking constantly. Return mixture to stockpot and cook over very low heat, stirring constantly, until thickened. Do not boil or soup will curdle. Ladle into soup bowls or small tea cups or soufflé dishes and garnish with lemon slices and chopped nuts.

CHICKEN AND WHITE BEAN SOUP

An aromatic chicken and vegetable soup makes a wonderful meal with a salad and crusty bread.

1 medium onion, diced
3 leeks, white part only, chopped
1 tsp. olive oil
2 cloves garlic, minced
1 qt. chicken stock
6 chicken thighs
1 tbs. Dijon mustard
1/3 cup dry white wine

1/2 lb. baby carrots, peeled
1 can (16 oz.) white beans, rinsed and
    drained
2 tbs. chopped fresh flat-leaf parsley
1 tsp. fresh thyme leaves, or 1/4 tsp.
    dried
salt and freshly ground pepper to taste

In a large saucepan over medium heat, sauté onion and leeks in oil for about 5 minutes, until soft. Add garlic, stock, chicken, mustard and wine. Cover and simmer for 30 minutes. Add carrots and beans and simmer for 15 minutes, or until chicken is tender. Add parsley, thyme, salt and pepper. Remove chicken from pot and cool slightly. Remove skin and bones from chicken and pull meat into large strips with your hands. Discard skin and bones. Return chicken meat to soup and heat through. Ladle into soup bowls.

CHICKEN SOUP WITH PESTO

Servings: 6

A rich chicken soup laced with vegetables and showered with Gruyère cheese and pesto offers a rewarding entrée for a winter repast. Use either homemade or commercially prepared pesto.

1½ qt. low-fat chicken stock, or 1½ qt.
    water plus 6 chicken bouillon cubes
1 onion, quartered
¼ cup celery leaves
1 broiler-fryer, about 3-3½ lb.
salt and freshly ground pepper to taste
4 carrots, sliced

2 leeks, chopped
1 stalk celery, chopped
2 medium turnips, peeled and diced
pesto
1 cup (4 oz.) shredded Gruyère or
    Jarlsberg cheese

In a large stockpot, bring stock to a boil. Add onion, celery leaves and whole chicken. Season with salt and pepper, cover and simmer for 1 hour, or until chicken is cooked through. Remove chicken from pot and cool slightly. Remove skin and bones from chicken and cut meat into large strips. Discard skin and bones. Strain stock and skim fat from the surface. Bring skimmed stock to a boil and add carrots, leeks, celery and turnips. Cover and simmer for 15 minutes, or until vegetables are crisp-tender. Add chicken strips and heat through. Ladle into soup bowls and pass bowls of pesto and cheese separately.

RANCHERO SOUP

This soup makes a swift-to-assemble starter for a South-of-the-Border menu.

4 cups richly flavored low-fat chicken stock
dash Tabasco Sauce
1 cup shredded cooked chicken
2 green onions, with half of the green tops, chopped
8 cherry tomatoes, chopped
1/3 cup chopped fresh cilantro
1 small avocado, peeled and diced
2 tbs. roasted pumpkin seeds or sunflower kernels
tortilla chips

In a medium saucepan, heat stock, Tabasco, chicken and onion over medium heat for about 2 to 3 minutes, or until hot. Stir in tomatoes, cilantro, avocado and pumpkin or sunflower seeds and ladle into soup bowls. Accompany with tortilla chips.

MOROCCAN MEATBALL SOUP

Chopped cilantro and tomatoes enliven this spicy full-meal soup. It's a marvelous meal by itself accompanied by crusty bread and sliced pears or grapes.

1 lb. ground chicken
3 tbs. cornstarch
1 egg or 2 egg whites
3 tbs. minced fresh cilantro
1 clove garlic, minced
1/4 tsp. salt
freshly ground pepper to taste
1 tsp. olive oil
1 onion, chopped
1 carrot, peeled and grated
1 stalk fennel or celery, chopped

5 cups richly-flavored low-fat chicken
    stock
1 tsp. grated fresh ginger
1/2 tsp. ground cumin
salt and freshly ground pepper to taste
3 tbs. tomato paste
1 cup shredded Swiss chard leaves,
    optional
2 Roma tomatoes, peeled and chopped,
    for garnish
1/4 cup chopped fresh cilantro for garnish

In a bowl, mix chicken, cornstarch, egg, 3 tbs. cilantro, garlic, ¼ tsp. salt and pepper until well blended; shape mixture into ¾-inch balls; set aside.

In a large saucepan over medium heat, heat oil and sauté onion, carrot and fennel in oil until soft. Add stock, ginger, cumin, salt, pepper and tomato paste. Cover and simmer for 25 minutes. Drop in meatballs and Swiss chard, if using, and cook for 10 to 15 minutes, or until meatballs are cooked through. Garnish with chopped tomatoes and cilantro just before serving. Ladle into soup bowls.

EARLY CALIFORNIA SOUP

This colorful soup/stew makes a full-meal dinner. Accompany with crispy tortilla chips and a sliced orange and jicama salad.

1 onion, chopped
1 tsp. olive oil
6 chicken drumsticks or thighs, skinned
1 qt. water
few celery leaves, chopped
2 cloves garlic, minced
salt and freshly ground pepper to taste
½ tsp. ground cumin
½ tsp. dried oregano
small piece red chile pepper, optional

1 ear corn cut into 1-inch slices or
    kernels removed
2 small yellow crookneck squash, sliced
2 small zucchini, sliced
¼ cup chopped fresh cilantro
2 tbs. roasted sunflower kernels
1 small avocado, peeled and diced
1 small red bell pepper, seeded and
    diced, optional

In a large stockpot, sauté onion in oil until soft. Add chicken, water, celery leaves, garlic, salt, pepper, cumin, oregano and chile, if using. Cover and simmer for 45 minutes to 1 hour, or until chicken is tender. Lift chicken from broth, remove and discard skin and bones and tear meat into strips. Skim fat from the surface of broth. Bring to a boil and add vegetables; simmer for 2 minutes. Add chicken and heat through. Ladle into soup bowls and sprinkle with remaining ingredients.

ROOTS AND SHOOTS CHICKEN SOUP

Servings: 4

Assorted vegetables, both roots and greens, enrich this healthy full-meal soup. It's a great way to utilize leftover roasted chicken. If desired, add a splash of dry white wine for a special lift just before serving.

4 dried porcini or shiitake mushrooms
½ cup water
1 qt. richly flavored low-fat chicken stock
2 leeks, white part only, sliced
2 carrots, sliced
2 turnips or parsnips, peeled and sliced
1½ tbs. cornstarch
1½ tbs. cold water

½ bunch spinach, leaves only, cut into
    ½-inch strips
½ head butter lettuce, cut into ½-inch
    strips
2 cups cooked chicken strips
2 tbs. chopped fresh flat-leaf parsley for
    garnish

Soak mushrooms in cold water for 15 minutes. Remove mushrooms and chop, reserving liquid. In a stockpot, bring chicken stock to a boil. Add mushroom liquid, chopped mushrooms, leeks, carrots and turnips. Cover and simmer for 15 to 20 minutes, or until vegetables are tender. Mix cornstarch and water together to form a paste and stir into soup. Add spinach, lettuce and chicken and heat through. Ladle into large soup bowls and sprinkle with parsley.

MIZUTAKI

This popular Japanese dish is not only delicious, but healthful as well. It is important to master the art of dining with chopsticks to enjoy it fully, as guests cook their own meal in the chicken stock. You'll need a Mongolian cooker or electric hot pot for tableside cooking and dining.

2 qt. chicken stock
3 boneless, skinless chicken breast halves, cut into 1-inch pieces
5 boneless, skinless chicken thighs, cut into 1-inch pieces

VEGETABLES
6 green onions, cut into 1-inch pieces
4 slender carrots, cut on the diagonal
1/2 lb. small white mushrooms
3/4 lb. spinach leaves
1/2 lb. snow peas, asparagus tips or broccoli florets

SAUCE
1/4 cup low-sodium soy sauce
1/4 cup sake (rice wine)
2 tbs. lemon juice

Place a Mongolian cooker or hot pot at the table within reach of all diners. Add chicken stock and heat until steaming. Assemble chicken on a tray with bowls of prepared vegetables. When stock is hot, add some vegetables and chicken and cook for about 3 to 5 minutes, or until chicken is cooked through. Remove cooked items with long chopsticks. Dip into sauce. When chicken and vegetables are gone, turn off the heat of cooker or hot pot and ladle stock into small cups for sipping, adding remaining sauce as desired.

THAI LEMON GRASS SOUP

Clean, scintillating seasonings uplift the flavor of this quick and delightful Far Eastern soup.

3 cups richly-flavored low-fat chicken stock
2 tsp. low-sodium soy sauce
dash hot pepper sauce
2 tsp. finely diced lemon grass
2 slices fresh ginger
¾ cup diced cooked chicken
2 green onions, finely chopped
6 white mushrooms, sliced
2 tbs. chopped fresh basil
1½ tbs. minced fresh mint

In a medium saucepan, heat stock, soy sauce, hot pepper sauce, lemon grass and ginger and simmer for 5 to 10 minutes. Add chicken, onions and mushrooms and heat through. Stir in basil and mint. Ladle into small soup bowls.

SALADS

PAPAYA, AVOCADO AND CHICKEN SALAD

Servings: 2

Papaya and avocado are natural partners and taste terrific with a lemon tarragon dressing. For a delectable variation, substitute sliced blood oranges and navel oranges for the papaya. If nasturtiums are blooming in the garden, tuck a blossom on each plate.

2 boneless, skinless chicken breast
   halves
1 tbs. fruity olive oil
1 tbs. lemon juice
salt and freshly ground pepper to taste
2 tbs. extra virgin olive oil
1 tbs. lemon juice
1 tbs. white wine vinegar
½ tsp. grated fresh lemon peel (zest)

¼ tsp. Dijon mustard
1 tsp. chopped fresh tarragon, or
   ¼ tsp. dried
salt and freshly ground pepper to taste
3 cups mixed salad greens
1 small papaya, peeled, halved, seeded
   and sliced
1 small avocado, peeled and sliced

Heat broiler or grill to high. With a mallet, flatten chicken breasts slightly to equal thickness. Drizzle chicken breasts with 1 tbs. oil and 1 tbs. lemon juice and sprinkle with salt and pepper. Grill or broil for 3 to 4 minutes per side, or until cooked through; slice into strips. Stir together 2 tbs. olive oil, 1 tbs. lemon juice, vinegar, lemon peel, mustard, tarragon, salt and pepper; toss with greens and arrange on 2 dinner plates. Top greens with papaya and avocado slices. Arrange warm chicken strips over all.

ISLAND CHICKEN SALAD IN PAPAYA BOATS

Servings: 2

Papaya halves make delicious shells for a salad medley. Or, use zigzag-cut cantaloupe halves or fanned mango slices for the chutney-laced chicken mixture.

2 tbs. sour cream
2 tbs. plain yogurt
1½ tsp. lime juice
1½ tsp. frozen orange juice
   concentrate, thawed
1 tbs. apricot or mango chutney
2 cooked boneless, skinless chicken
   breast halves

1 tbs. lime juice
½ cup diced celery hearts or fennel bulb
¾ cup seedless red or green grapes
oak leaf or butter lettuce leaves
1 small papaya, peeled, halved and
   seeded
2 tbs. chopped macadamia or pistachio
   nuts for garnish

Mix together sour cream, yogurt, 1½ tsp. lime juice, juice concentrate and chutney; set aside. Cut chicken into strips or cubes and drizzle with 1 tbs. lime juice. Place in a bowl with celery hearts and grapes. Add chutney dressing and mix lightly. Arrange lettuce on serving plates. Spoon salad into papaya halves. Place filled papaya halves on lettuce and sprinkle with nuts.

ASIAN CHICKEN AND FRUIT SALAD

Sliced kiwi fruits and oranges make a refreshing counterpoint to chicken and a sesame-soy dressing. Cantaloupe or honeydew melon slices can substitute for the oranges.

2 tbs. canola oil
1 tbs. light soy sauce
1 tbs. sesame oil
1 tbs. lemon juice or raspberry vinegar
2 tsp. honey
½ tsp. grated fresh lemon peel (zest)
dash hot pepper sauce, optional
2 cooked boneless, skinless chicken
    breast halves

butter lettuce leaves or mixed salad
    greens
2 navel oranges, thinly sliced
2 kiwi fruits, peeled and thinly sliced
½ cup blueberries or raspberries
2 tbs. toasted slivered almonds or
    pistachio nuts for garnish

In a bowl, stir together canola oil, soy sauce, sesame oil, lemon juice, honey, lemon peel and hot pepper sauce, if using; set aside. Tear chicken into strips. Place chicken in a bowl and toss with ½ of the sesame-soy dressing. Arrange lettuce on serving plates and arrange semicircles of orange and kiwi fruit slices on top. Scatter chicken and berries over lettuce. Sprinkle with nuts and drizzle with remaining dressing.

CHICKEN WALDORF SALAD

Servings: 4

You can use either poached, roasted or barbecued chicken strips to update and enhance a classic Waldorf salad. For a beautiful presentation, cut the apples and chicken into pieces that are the same size.

2 green apples, such as Granny Smith
1 red apple, such as Gala or Braeburn
2 tbs. lemon juice
¾ cup sliced celery
2 cups cooked chicken pieces (½-inch cubes or strips)
½ cup coarsely chopped toasted walnuts or pecans

¼ cup dried cranberries, cherries or golden raisins
¼ cup mayonnaise
¼ cup plain yogurt
2 tsp. chopped fresh tarragon, or ½ tsp. dried
1 tsp. honey
butter lettuce or red oak leaf lettuce

Core and quarter apples and slice or dice. Place in a bowl and toss with 1 tbs. of the lemon juice. Add celery, chicken pieces, nuts and cranberries. Mix together mayonnaise, yogurt, remaining 1 tbs. lemon juice, tarragon and honey and mix with chicken mixture. Arrange lettuce on serving plates and spoon salad over the top.

CHARCOAL-GRILLED CUMIN CHICKEN AND ORANGE SALAD

Servings: 4

When fresh navel oranges are in season, this makes a colorful winter salad. Include a blood orange for extra tang and a pretty splash of color.

4 boneless, skinless chicken breast halves
4 tsp. cumin seeds
1½ cups plain yogurt
salt and freshly ground pepper to taste
1 tbs. chopped fresh mint, basil or
    cilantro leaves
4-5 tbs. fresh orange juice
2 tbs. olive oil
3-4 cups salad greens: baby spinach, curly
    endive and/or red leaf lettuce
2-3 oranges, peeled and sectioned
fresh mint, basil or cilantro sprigs for garnish

Place chicken between 2 sheets of plastic wrap and pound lightly with a mallet to an even thickness. In a large skillet over medium heat, toast cumin seeds, tossing constantly for about 3 minutes, until light brown. Transfer to a plate and cool; pulverize with a mortar and pestle or spice grinder. Rub chicken lightly with about 2 tsp. of the cumin. Combine ¾ cup of the yogurt with 1 tsp. of the cumin, salt, pepper and chopped herb. Pour over chicken in a bowl, cover and refrigerate for 2 hours or longer. Warm chicken to room temperature before grilling.

Prepare a medium-hot barbecue fire. Brush off excess marinade from chicken and grill for about 4 to 5 minutes per side, or until cooked through. Mix 2 tbs. of the orange juice with olive oil and use to baste chicken during grilling. Cool cooked chicken to room temperature and remove skin. With your hands, shred chicken into bite-sized pieces.

For dressing, combine remaining ¾ cup yogurt with 1 tsp. ground cumin, salt, pepper and 2 to 3 tbs. of the orange juice.

To serve, tear crisped greens into generous bite-sized pieces and toss with enough dressing to coat lightly. Mound on individual plates. Nestle chicken and orange sections on and between lettuce leaves. Garnish with mint, basil or cilantro sprigs.

CRANBERRY, WHEAT BERRY AND CHICKEN SALAD

Wheat berries, which are whole wheat kernels, yield a delicious nutty crunch with tart-sweet cranberries in this refreshing entrée salad. Wheat berries are high in fiber, rich in protein and available in bulk food bins. If you can't find wheat berries, cooked brown rice can stand in. Wheat berries demand a lengthy cooking time, but they can be done ahead and frozen.

1 cup wheat berries
3 cups boiling salted water
Balsamic-Orange Vinaigrette, follows
⅓ cup dried cranberries or golden raisins
arugula or spinach leaves
3 blood or navel oranges, peeled and sliced
4 cooked boneless, skinless chicken thighs,
    cut into strips
3 tbs. coarsely chopped pistachio nuts or
    toasted almonds for garnish

Toast wheat berries in a dry skillet over medium-high heat for 2 minutes. In a medium saucepan, cook wheat berries in boiling salted water for 1½ to 2 hours, or until just tender, but still have a slight bite. Drain off any liquid. Stir in vinaigrette, cover and chill. When ready to serve, toss salad with cranberries and transfer to a platter lined with arugula or spinach leaves. Ring with oranges and chicken. Sprinkle with nuts.

BALSAMIC-ORANGE VINAIGRETTE
2 tbs. balsamic vinegar
2 tbs. orange juice
1 tbs. walnut oil or olive oil
1 tbs. slivered fresh orange peel (zest)
½ tsp. ground allspice
1 tsp. Dijon mustard
⅓ cup finely diced red onion or shallot

In a covered jar, shake ingredients together until blended.

CURRIED COUSCOUS AND CHICKEN SALAD

Servings: 4-6

Couscous, made from milling durum or hard wheat, expands in minutes to a soft consistency once moistened with hot broth or water. You can find this grain in a package or in bulk bins. Chicken, dried apricots and pistachios lend a special flourish to couscous that is bound with a curried yogurt dressing. For an even more dramatic presentation, omit adding the chicken to the couscous; instead, accompany it with grilled chicken kebabs.

1½ cups chicken stock
1 cup couscous
Curried Yogurt Dressing, follows
2 cooked boneless, skinless chicken breast halves, cut into ½-inch strips
1 cup thinly sliced celery
½ cup chopped dried apricots
½ lb. sugar snap peas, steamed and cut on the diagonal
3 green onions, chopped
romaine lettuce leaves
3 tbs. chopped pistachio nuts for garnish
chopped fresh cilantro for garnish

In a saucepan, bring stock to a boil and stir in couscous; remove from heat and let stand until liquid is absorbed and couscous is tender. Cool to room temperature. With a fork, stir couscous to separate grains. Stir in dressing, chicken, celery and apricots. Cover and refrigerate for 2 hours or longer. Just before serving, mix in sugar snap peas and green onions. Line a platter with romaine leaves and spoon salad on top. Garnish with nuts and cilantro.

CURRIED YOGURT DRESSING

1 cup plain yogurt
2 tbs. mango chutney
2 tbs. lemon juice
2 tsp. curry powder
¼ tsp. ground allspice
¼ tsp. dry mustard

Stir all ingredients together in a bowl.

LEMON GRASS COUSCOUS SALAD
WITH CHICKEN AND GRAPES

Lemon grass and cilantro lend an intriguing flavor to couscous for a chicken salad entrée.

½ cup couscous or medium-fine
   cracked wheat
¾ cup boiling water
¾ cup cilantro sprigs
2 cloves garlic, minced
3 tbs. pistachio nuts
1 tbs. chopped lemon grass, or 2 tsp.
   grated fresh lemon peel (zest)
2 tbs. fruity olive oil

1 tbs. lime or lemon juice
assorted greens: butter lettuce, red oak
   leaf lettuce and/or radicchio
2 cooked boneless, skinless chicken breast
   halves, or 3 thighs, cut into strips
1 cup seedless red or green grapes
chopped fresh cilantro for garnish

Place couscous in a bowl and add boiling water. Cover and let stand for 10 minutes, until cooled to room temperature. In a blender container, place cilantro sprigs, garlic, nuts, lemon grass, olive oil and lime juice and process just until finely minced. Add to couscous and mix lightly with a fork to separate grains. Line each of 2 dinner plates with greens. Mound salad on top of greens. Ring with chicken and grapes and garnish with chopped cilantro.

LENTIL, CHICKEN AND APRICOT SALAD

The nutty bite of green lentils and the sweet-tart flavor of dried apricots pair with chicken and a balsamic-raspberry vinaigrette in this savory main-dish salad. You can vary the fruit accent with the season, substituting 2 sliced oranges or red Bartlett pears for the grapes.

2 tbs. balsamic vinegar
2 tbs. raspberry vinegar
1 tbs. olive oil
1 tsp. Dijon mustard
1/3 cup finely diced red onion or shallots
1 cup French green or other lentils
3 cups boiling salted water
1/2 cup chopped dried apricots

2 green onions, with half of the green tops, chopped
salad greens
1 1/2 cups seedless red or green grapes
2 cooked boneless, skinless chicken breast halves, cut into strips
3 tbs. coarsely chopped pistachio nuts or pine nuts for garnish

In a covered jar, shake vinegars, oil, mustard and onion together until well blended; set aside. In a saucepan, cook lentils in boiling salted water for 25 minutes, or until just tender, but with a slight bite, *al dente*. Drain any liquid. Stir in dressing, apricots and green onions, cover and refrigerate. When ready to serve, transfer salad to a platter lined with greens and ring with grapes and chicken. Sprinkle with nuts.

WILD RICE, WHITE CORN AND CHICKEN SALAD

This colorful combination makes a glorious full-meal salad for a picnic or potluck gathering. Cook extra chicken breasts for this salad a day in advance.

3 cups water
1 tsp. salt
1 cup wild rice
kernels from 3 ears fresh white corn
4 cooked boneless, skinless chicken breast
    halves, cut into ½-inch strips, or 2½ cups
    grilled or roasted chicken strips
⅓ cup oil-packed sun-dried tomatoes, chopped
Balsamic Vinaigrette, follows
¼ cup toasted pine nuts
salad greens
¼ cup slivered fresh basil leaves for garnish
fresh basil sprigs for garnish

In a large saucepan, bring water to a boil and add salt and wild rice. Reduce heat to low, cover and simmer for 45 minutes, or until rice is tender, but with a slight bite, *al dente*. Drain any excess water and cool. In a bowl, toss together cooled rice, corn kernels, chicken, tomatoes, *Balsamic Vinaigrette* and nuts. Line a platter or shallow bowl with greens and mound salad on top. Sprinkle with basil and basil sprigs.

BALSAMIC VINAIGRETTE
3 tbs. canola oil
1 tbs. dark sesame oil or walnut oil
2 tbs. balsamic vinegar
1 tbs. red wine vinegar
1/2 tsp. Dijon mustard
1 shallot, chopped
salt and freshly ground pepper to taste

In a covered jar, shake together all ingredients until well blended.

CHICKEN AND POTATO SALAD CAESAR

The pungent accents of garlic, Parmesan cheese and anchovies lend verve to this full-meal salad. A fresh peach or apple tart or crisp might follow for dessert.

2 cloves garlic, minced
1/4 cup extra virgin olive oil
1 1/2 lb. small Yukon Gold or red new potatoes
1/3 cup dry white wine
1 cup sweet or sourdough French bread cubes (1/2-inch cubes)
2 tbs. balsamic vinegar
2 tbs. lemon juice
2 tsp. Dijon mustard
2 tsp. anchovy paste
salt and freshly ground pepper to taste
2 shallots or green onions, white part only, chopped
2 cooked boneless, skinless chicken breast halves, cut into 1/4-inch strips
inner leaves of 1 head Romaine or red leaf lettuce
1/4 cup (1 oz.) freshly grated Parmesan cheese

Steep garlic in oil for 30 minutes and discard garlic. Halve potatoes and steam over simmering water for 15 to 18 minutes, or until just tender when pierced with a knife. Transfer potatoes to a bowl and, when cool enough to handle, cut into ¼-inch-thick slices. Add wine and toss gently. Cool.

Heat oven to 350°. Toss bread cubes with 1 tbs. of the garlic oil, place in a baking pan and bake for 10 minutes, or until golden brown; cool. Mix remaining garlic oil with vinegar, lemon juice, mustard, anchovy paste, salt and pepper; pour over potatoes. Add shallots and chicken and toss gently. Cover and refrigerate. At serving time, arrange leaves of lettuce on a platter and mound salad over the top. Sprinkle with toasted bread cubes and cheese.

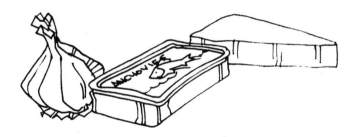

GRILLED CHICKEN AND
ROASTED VEGETABLE SALAD

This makes a pretty summer salad entrée. If desired, grill extra chicken breasts and vegetables one night to enjoy the leftovers cold in this salad the next night. The vegetables can be grilled instead of roasted, if desired.

$\frac{1}{3}$ cup dry red wine
1 tbs. olive oil
1 tbs. fresh rosemary leaves, or $\frac{3}{4}$ tsp. dried
1 clove garlic, minced
1 lb. boneless chicken breasts or thighs, skin removed if desired
2 tbs. fruity olive oil
1 clove garlic, minced
2 tsp. chopped fresh rosemary, or $\frac{1}{2}$ tsp. dried
2 Japanese eggplants, sliced diagonally
2 medium zucchini, sliced diagonally
1 red bell pepper, halved, seeded and cut into strips
1 gold bell pepper, halved, seeded and cut into strips
1 red onion, cut into wedges
3 cups mixed baby salad greens
4 sprigs rosemary for garnish

Combine wine, 1 tbs. olive oil, 1 tbs. rosemary leaves and 1 clove garlic in a large bowl. Add chicken and marinate in the refrigerator for at least 1 hour.

Heat oven to 425°. Mix 2 tbs. oil with 1 clove minced garlic and 2 tsp. rosemary. Place vegetables in a roasting pan and brush with oil mixture. Roast for 20 to 25 minutes, or until just cooked through; cool.

Prepare a hot barbecue fire or heat grill or broiler to high. Remove chicken from marinade and grill or broil for 3 to 4 minutes per side, or until cooked through; cook thighs a few minutes longer. Cool and slice thinly.

To assemble, arrange greens on each of 4 plates and top with chicken. Arrange vegetables alongside chicken. Garnish with rosemary sprigs.

GRILLED CHICKEN SALAD NIÇOISE

Chicken gives a boost to the classic niçoise salad. New potatoes are a particularly good choice to use.

1 lb. small red new potatoes, about 1¼ inches in diameter
¼ cup dry white wine or vermouth
½ lb. tiny green beans, trimmed and cut into 2-inch pieces
2 boneless, skinless chicken breast halves
2 tsp. Dijon mustard
salt and freshly ground pepper to taste
Shallot Vinaigrette, follows
leaf lettuce
1 cup cherry tomatoes, halved
2 hard-cooked eggs, quartered
12 niçoise olives, pitted, for garnish
2 tbs. minced fresh flat-leaf parsley for garnish

Place whole potatoes in a steamer basket and steam over simmering water for 15 to 20 minutes, or until fork-tender. Cut potatoes into ¼-inch-thick slices, leaving on peel, place in a bowl and pour wine over potatoes. Place beans in steamer basket and steam over simmering water for 5 to 7 minutes, or until crisp-tender; chill under cold running water and drain.

Heat broiler. Brush chicken with mustard and sprinkle with salt and pepper. Place chicken on a broiling pan and broil for about 3 to 4 minutes per side, or until cooked through. Cool chicken slightly and cut into ½-inch strips.

In a large bowl, mix potatoes and green beans gently with *Shallot Vinaigrette*. Arrange greens on each of 3 to 4 dinner plates and mound potato-bean mixture on top. Place chicken in a strip down the center of each plate and arrange tomatoes and eggs on either side. Garnish with olives and parsley.

SHALLOT VINAIGRETTE

1 tsp. Dijon mustard
2 tbs. tarragon wine vinegar
2 tbs. olive oil

2 cloves garlic, minced
2 tbs. chopped shallot
1 tsp. anchovy paste, optional

Mix all ingredients together in a bowl.

VIETNAMESE PICK-UP SALAD

This taste-tingling salad gets rolled up in spinach leaves to savor out of hand. The wonderful interplay of mint, cilantro, chile and ginger punctuates it with vibrancy, Vietnamese-style. Look for nuoc mam and cellophane noodles in the Asian section of your supermarket.

1 clove garlic, minced
1 tsp. minced fresh ginger
1/8 tsp. red chile flakes
2 tsp. sugar
2 tbs. fresh lemon or lime juice
1/4 cup unseasoned rice vinegar
2 tbs. nuoc mam (fish sauce)
1 tsp. canola oil
1 clove garlic, minced
1 green onion, white part only, chopped
3/4 lb. coarsely ground uncooked
    chicken breast

1 tbs. light soy sauce
2 large carrots, grated
2 tsp. grated fresh ginger
1 cup finely diced cucumber
1 cup bean sprouts or plumped
    cellophane noodles
3 tbs. chopped fresh mint leaves
1/2 cup fresh cilantro leaves
1 bunch spinach, stems removed

In a small bowl, stir together 1 clove garlic, 1 tsp. fresh ginger, red chile flakes, sugar, lemon juice, rice vinegar and nuoc mam; set aside.

In a large skillet over medium heat, heat oil and sauté 1 clove garlic and onion for 1 minute. Add chicken and cook until browned and crumbly. Sprinkle with soy sauce and remove from heat. In a large bowl, toss carrots with 2 tsp. ginger. Add cucumber, bean sprouts, mint and cilantro and mix lightly. Add dressing and toss to combine.

Ring a platter with spinach leaves and mound salad in the center. To eat, fill spinach leaves with salad, roll up and eat.

NOTE: To plump and soften cellophane noodles, pour boiling water over noodles in a bowl and let stand until cool; drain.

CHICKEN, MUSHROOM AND FENNEL SALAD

Servings: 4

Anise-flavored fennel, creamy cheese and woodsy mushrooms mingle with chicken for an intriguing salad combo.

1/4 cup olive oil
2 tbs. lemon juice
1 tsp. Dijon mustard
1/2 tsp. grated fresh lemon peel (zest)
salt and pepper to taste
1 tsp. chopped fresh tarragon, or
   1/4 tsp. dried
1/2 lb. white mushrooms, thinly sliced
1 cup thinly sliced fennel bulb

2 cups cooked chicken strips
1/4 lb. Gruyère or Jarlsberg cheese, cut
   into matchstick strips
butter lettuce leaves
1 cup cherry tomatoes, halved
2 tbs. chopped pistachio nuts
   for garnish
2 tbs. chopped fresh parsley for garnish

In a small bowl, mix together olive oil, lemon juice, mustard, lemon peel, salt, pepper and tarragon. In a large bowl, place mushrooms, fennel and chicken. Stir in dressing, cover and chill for 1 hour, mixing once or twice. Mix in cheese. Spoon onto a platter or plates lined with lettuce and ring with cherry tomatoes. Sprinkle with nuts and parsley.

SOUTHWEST SUMMER SALAD

Leftover grilled chicken breasts make a tasty comeback in this colorful entrée salad. Accompany with warm cornbread or rolled flour tortillas.

2 navel oranges
1 sweet red onion
3 cooked boneless, skinless chicken
   breast halves, cut into 1/2-inch strips
1/2 cup matchstick strips jicama
1/2 cup matchstick strips red bell pepper
1/4 cup canola oil
3 tbs. orange juice

1 tbs. white wine vinegar
1 tbs. lime or lemon juice
1/4 tsp. ground cumin
1/4 tsp. dry mustard
salt and freshly ground pepper to taste
dash hot pepper sauce, optional
salad greens
cilantro sprigs for garnish

Peel and thinly slice oranges and onion. Place in a bowl with chicken, jicama and red pepper. Mix together oil, orange juice, vinegar, lime juice, cumin, mustard, salt and pepper. Add hot pepper sauce, if desired. Pour over salad. Cover and chill for 1 hour. Arrange greens on a platter, spoon salad mixture on top and garnish with cilantro.

PIZZAS AND PASTAS

ARMENIAN CHICKEN TORTILLA PIZZAS

Servings: 2

Big flour tortillas make neat, fast pizza bases for plate-sized chicken and mushroom pizzas. Leftover grilled, broiled or roasted chicken is smart to use for this dish.

two 9- or 10-inch flour tortillas
6 tbs. roasted garlic- or pesto-flavored tomato paste
½ tsp. dried oregano
¼ tsp. ground allspice
2 cooked boneless, skinless chicken thighs, cut into strips
3 green onions, with half of the green tops, chopped
¼ lb. white mushrooms, sliced
2 tbs. pine nuts
½ cup (2 oz.) shredded Monterey Jack cheese

Heat oven to 425°. Place tortillas on baking sheets. Spread tortillas with tomato paste, leaving a ¾-inch border. Sprinkle with oregano and allspice and scatter chicken, green onions, mushrooms, nuts and cheese over the top. Bake for 10 to 12 minutes, or until the edges are crisp. Cut into wedges to serve.

CHICKEN, PEPPER AND PEAR TORTILLA PIZZAS

Servings: 2

Red bell peppers and pears make a wonderful duo with chicken in these quick-to-assemble pizzas.

two 9- or 10-inch flour tortillas
6 tbs. roasted garlic-flavored tomato paste
1/4 tsp. ground allspice
2 cooked boneless, skinless chicken thighs, cut into strips
3 green onions, with half of the green tops, chopped
1 Anjou or Bosc pear, sliced
1/2 cup diced red bell pepper
2 tbs. pistachio nuts
1/2 cup (2 oz.) shredded Gruyère or Jarlsberg cheese

Heat oven to 425°. Place tortillas on baking sheets. Spread tortillas with tomato paste, leaving a 3/4-inch border. Sprinkle with allspice and scatter chicken, green onions, pear, pepper, nuts and cheese over the top. Bake for 10 to 12 minutes, or until the edges are crisp. Cut into wedges to serve.

CHICKEN AND GRAPE PITA PIZZAS

Servings: 2-4

These novel individual pizzas are swift to create using split pita breads. The combination of chutney, grapes and chicken makes a delicious topping on these cheese-laced hot breads.

two 7-inch whole wheat pita breads
1/2 cup ricotta cheese
1/3 cup mango chutney
2 cooked boneless, skinless chicken breast halves, cut into 1/2-inch strips
2 green onions, with half of the green tops, chopped
1 oz. thinly sliced good-quality ham, cut into matchstick strips
1 1/2 cups seedless green or red grapes
2 tbs. pistachio nuts, optional
1/4 cup (1 oz.) shredded Jarlsberg or Monterey Jack cheese

Heat oven to 425°. Carefully split pita breads, making 4 disks. Place disks on a baking sheet. Combine ricotta cheese with chutney and spread over disks. Scatter chicken, onions, ham, grapes, nuts and shredded cheese over ricotta mixture. Bake for about 6 minutes, or until the edges are crisp. Cut into wedges to serve.

BARBECUED CHICKEN PIZZA

Choose a favorite barbecue sauce, one as hot and spicy as you like, for this crusty pizza. A smart plan is to grill the chicken a day ahead and reserve some extra for this topping. For a short-cut version, substitute commercially prepared pizza crusts for the homemade dough.

PIZZA DOUGH
2 tsp. active dry yeast
1 cup lukewarm water (105°-115°)
1 tsp. honey or granulated sugar
2½ cups unbleached all-purpose flour
¾ tsp. salt
2 tbs. extra virgin olive oil

TOPPING
4 boneless, skinless chicken breasts
1½ cups barbecue sauce
2 cups (8 oz.) shredded Gouda or fontina cheese
1 sweet red onion, thinly sliced and separated into rings
3 tbs. chopped fresh oregano or cilantro

For pizza dough, sprinkle yeast over water in a large bowl and stir in honey. Let stand for about 10 minutes, or until yeast is dissolved and mixture is puffy. Mix in 1 cup of the flour, salt and oil, mixing with a wooden spoon or with a dough hook in a heavy duty mixer, until smooth. Gradually add remaining flour, mixing until dough clings together in a ball. Transfer dough to a floured board and knead until smooth and elastic, about 5 minutes. If you use a heavy duty mixer, mix for 5 minutes instead of kneading on a board. Place dough in an oiled bowl, turn to coat dough ball with oil and cover with plastic wrap. Let dough rise in a warm, draft-free place (70° to 80°) for about 1½ hours, or until doubled in size.

In a locking plastic bag, marinate chicken in ½ cup of the barbecue sauce in the refrigerator for 2 hours or longer. Prepare a hot barbecue fire or heat grill or broiler to high. Remove chicken from marinade and grill or broil for about 3 minutes per side, or until cooked through. Cool and cut into bite-sized pieces.

At least 20 minutes before baking, heat oven to 475°. Remove dough from bowl and knead lightly on a floured board. With a rolling pin, roll dough into a 14-inch disk and place on an oiled 14-inch pizza pan. Top with cheese, remaining barbecue sauce, chicken and onion rings. Let rise for 20 minutes. Bake for 15 minutes, or until golden brown underneath and crispy. Garnish with fresh oregano. Cut into wedges to serve.

CHICKEN AND SUN-DRIED TOMATO PIZZA

For a shortcut, you can use a Boboli pizza crust or a 1-pound package of frozen bread dough, thawed, for this herb-scented chicken pizza.

Pizza Dough, page 66
1 tbs. olive oil
4 boneless, skinless chicken thighs, cut into ½-inch strips
1 sweet red onion, thinly sliced and separated into rings
2 zucchini, sliced
salt and freshly ground pepper to taste
¾ cup oil-packed sun-dried tomatoes, drained and chopped
2 cups (8 oz.) shredded Italian fontina or Monterey Jack cheese
2 tbs. minced fresh basil
2 tbs. minced fresh sage or flat-leaf parsley
basil or sage leaves for garnish

Prepare *Pizza Dough*.

In a large skillet, heat oil over medium-high heat and sauté chicken for about 2 to 3 minutes, or until browned. Push chicken to one side of skillet, add onion and zucchini and sauté for 2 minutes. Season with salt and pepper and stir in sun-dried tomatoes.

At least 20 minutes before baking, heat oven to 475°. Remove dough from bowl and knead lightly on a floured board. With a rolling pin, roll dough into a 14-inch disk and place on an oiled 14-inch pizza pan. Top with chicken and vegetables and sprinkle with cheese. Let rise for 20 minutes. Bake for 15 minutes, or until golden brown underneath and crispy. Garnish with chopped fresh herbs and herb sprigs. Cut into wedges to serve.

PENNE WITH CHICKEN, ARTICHOKES AND SUN-DRIED TOMATOES

Sun-dried tomatoes and artichoke hearts bring a wonderful flavor impact to this chicken and pasta dish. A Caesar salad would make a choice starter. Why not finish off with coffee-flavored frozen yogurt and amaretti cookies?

10 oz. dried penne or other pasta
2 shallots or green onions, white part only, chopped
2 cloves garlic, minced
2 tbs. extra virgin olive oil
3 boneless, skinless chicken breast halves, cut into 1/2-inch strips
1/4 cup dry white wine
1 pkg. (8 oz.) frozen artichoke hearts, cooked, or 8 oz. fresh artichoke hearts, cooked, or 1 can (14 oz.) quartered artichoke hearts, drained
1/3 cup matchstick strips oil-packed sun-dried tomatoes
salt and freshly ground pepper to taste
3 tbs. minced fresh flat-leaf parsley for garnish
freshly grated Parmesan cheese for garnish

In a large pot of rapidly boiling salted water, cook pasta until slightly firm to the bite, *al dente*, about 8 to 10 minutes. While pasta is cooking, sauté shallots and garlic in 1 tbs. of the oil in a large skillet over medium heat, until soft. Add chicken and sauté for 2 to 3 minutes; add wine, artichoke hearts, sun-dried tomatoes, salt and pepper and simmer just until heated through. Drain pasta, leaving a little water clinging to it, and place in a warm serving dish. Toss with chicken mixture and sauce and garnish with parsley and cheese.

ROTELLE WITH CHICKEN AND SUMMER VEGETABLES

In the peak of the late-summer harvest season, fresh eggplant, zucchini and yellow summer squash are superb with dark chicken thighs and pasta twists.

10 oz. dried rotelle or other pasta shapes
1/4 cup chopped red onion
2 cloves garlic, minced
2 tbs. extra virgin olive oil
4 boneless, skinless chicken thighs,
    cut into 1/2-inch strips
1 small Japanese eggplant, diced
1 zucchini, thinly sliced

1 yellow squash, thinly sliced
1/4 cup dry red wine
1 tbs. pesto-flavored tomato paste
salt and freshly ground pepper to taste
3 tbs. minced fresh basil for garnish
3 tbs. minced fresh flat-leaf parsley for
    garnish
freshly grated Parmesan cheese for garnish

In a large pot of rapidly boiling salted water, cook pasta until slightly firm to the bite, *al dente*, about 8 to 10 minutes. While pasta is cooking, sauté onion and garlic in oil in a large nonstick skillet over medium heat until soft. Add chicken and sauté for 2 to 3 minutes. Add eggplant, zucchini and yellow squash and sauté for 2 minutes; add wine, tomato paste, salt and pepper and simmer just until chicken is cooked through. Drain pasta, leaving a little water clinging to it, and place in a warm serving dish. Toss with chicken and vegetable mixture and garnish with basil, parsley and cheese.

SPINACH PASTA WITH CHICKEN AND RED AND GOLD TOMATOES

Servings: 4

Vine-ripened red and gold plum tomatoes mingle with golden chicken strips and basil in this verdant pasta dish. Any leftovers are excellent served chilled the next day, refreshed with a splash of lemon juice and olive oil and tossed with fresh herbs.

10 oz. dried spinach fettuccine
2 shallots or green onions, white part
  only, chopped
1 clove garlic, minced
3 tbs. extra virgin olive oil
3 boneless, skinless chicken breast
  halves, cut into 1/2-inch strips

1 1/2 tbs. lemon juice
1 cup halved red and gold plum or
  cherry tomatoes
3 tbs. minced fresh flat-leaf parsley
3 tbs. minced fresh basil
salt and freshly ground pepper to taste
freshly grated Parmesan cheese for garnish

In a large pot of rapidly boiling salted water, cook pasta until slightly firm to the bite, *al dente*, about 8 to 10 minutes. While pasta is cooking, sauté shallots and garlic in 1 tbs. of the oil in a large skillet over medium heat until soft. Add chicken and sauté for 2 to 3 minutes. Add lemon juice, tomatoes, parsley and basil and heat through. Season with salt and pepper. Drain pasta, leaving a little water clinging to it, and place in a warm serving dish. Toss with remaining oil, chicken, tomatoes, salt and pepper. Sprinkle with grated cheese.

FETTUCCINE WITH CHICKEN, MUSHROOMS AND GOAT CHEESE

Goat cheese, pine nuts and mushrooms mingle for an elegant, fast pasta sauce.

10 oz. fresh or dried fettuccine
2 shallots, chopped
1 clove garlic, minced
3 tbs. extra virgin olive oil
3 boneless, skinless chicken breast
    halves, cut into 1/2-inch strips
1/2 lb. white mushrooms, sliced
1 1/2 tbs. lemon juice

2 tsp. grated fresh lemon peel (zest)
3 tbs. minced fresh flat-leaf parsley
freshly ground pepper to taste
3 oz. fresh goat cheese
3 tbs. lightly toasted pine nuts
freshly grated Gruyère or Parmesan
    cheese for garnish

In a large pot of rapidly boiling salted water, cook pasta until slightly firm to the bite, *al dente,* about 3 minutes for fresh pasta and 8 to 10 minutes for dried. While pasta is cooking, sauté shallots and garlic in 1 tbs. of the oil in a large nonstick skillet over medium heat until soft. Add chicken and sauté for 2 to 3 minutes. Add mushrooms and sauté over medium-high heat until just softened. Drain pasta, leaving a little water clinging to it, and place in a warm serving dish. Toss with remaining oil, lemon juice, zest, chicken mixture, parsley and pepper. Top with spoonfuls of goat cheese and pine nuts and toss again. Sprinkle with grated cheese.

CHICKEN AND SUGAR SNAP FETTUCCINE

Servings: 4

Pesto uplifts this tasty pasta dish. Consider accompanying it with a hearts of romaine salad and finish off with biscotti and grapes or strawberries.

1½ tbs. olive oil
3 boneless, skinless chicken breast halves, cut into ½-inch strips
3 green onions, with half of the green tops, chopped
6 oz. sugar snap peas or snow pea pods, ends trimmed and strings removed

3 tbs. pine nuts or pistachio nuts
¼ cup heavy cream
12 cherry tomatoes, halved
¼ cup pesto, homemade or purchased
10 oz. fresh fettuccine or tagliarini
freshly grated Romano cheese for garnish

In a large skillet over medium-high heat, heat oil and sauté chicken for 2 to 3 minutes, or until almost cooked through. Add onions and peas and cook for about 2 minutes, until softened. Push to one side of skillet. Add nuts and sauté until lightly browned. Add cream, tomatoes and pesto and heat through. Cook fettuccine in a large pot of rapidly boiling salted water for about 3 minutes, until slightly firm to the bite, *al dente*; drain. Spoon hot sauce over pasta, mix lightly and spoon onto warm dinner plates. Sprinkle with cheese.

CHICKEN WITH SOBA AND PEA PODS

Buckwheat noodles, called soba, are a flavorful treat tossed with chicken, pea pods and fresh herbs in this eclectic dish. Look for soba in a gourmet supermarket.

10 oz. soba noodles or dried fettuccine
2 shallots, chopped
1 clove garlic, minced
2 tbs. canola oil
3 boneless, skinless chicken breast
    halves, cut into ½-inch strips
¼ lb. snow pea pods, ends trimmed
    and strings removed

2 tbs. rice vinegar
1 tbs. soy sauce
2 tbs. rice wine or sherry
1 tbs. Asian sesame oil
¼ cup slivered fresh basil leaves
1 tbs. minced fresh mint

In a large pot of rapidly boiling salted water, cook pasta until slightly firm to the bite, *al dente*, about 8 minutes. While pasta is cooking, sauté shallots and garlic in oil in a large skillet over medium heat until soft. Add chicken and sauté for 3 to 4 minutes. Add pea pods and sauté over medium-high heat for 1 minute, or just until softened. Drain pasta, leaving a little water clinging to it, and place in a warm serving dish. Toss with vinegar, soy sauce, rice wine, sesame oil, chicken mixture, basil and mint.

LINGUINI WITH CHICKEN AND LEEKS

When tossed, the hot pasta melts the cheese in the savory leek sauce to gild the pasta strands.

10 oz. dried linguini
2 tbs. olive oil
3 boneless, skinless chicken breast
    halves, cut into 1/2-inch strips
3 leeks, white part only, chopped
1 egg yolk
1/4 cup heavy cream

2 oz. Brie, mascarpone or shredded
    fontina cheese, room temperature
1/4 cup (1 oz.) freshly grated Parmesan
    cheese, plus extra for passing
1/4 cup minced fresh flat-leaf parsley
salt and freshly ground pepper to taste

In a large pot of rapidly boiling salted water, cook pasta until slightly firm to the bite, *al dente*, about 8 to 10 minutes. In a large skillet over medium heat, heat 1 tbs. of the oil and sauté chicken for about 3 to 4 minutes, or until cooked through; transfer to a plate. Add leeks and remaining oil to skillet and cook until soft, about 6 to 8 minutes. In a warm shallow serving bowl, beat egg yolk and mix in cream, cheeses, parsley, salt, pepper, chicken and leeks. Add about 1/4 cup of the pasta cooking water to chicken-leek sauce. Drain pasta and toss with sauce. Pass extra grated cheese at the table.

CAPELLINI WITH CHICKEN AND PEANUT SAUCE

Cold noodles with spicy peanut sauce, Szechuan-style, is a healthy dish with a melange of shredded vegetables. Cabbage and jicama are other vegetables to consider shredding and including.

10 oz. capellini or spaghettini
2 tbs. chopped shallot
1 clove garlic, minced
2 tbs. canola oil
3 boneless, skinless chicken breast
    halves, cut into 1/2-inch strips
3 tbs. creamy peanut butter
2 tbs. water
1 tbs. toasted sesame oil

2 tbs. soy sauce
1 tbs. rice vinegar
2 tsp. brown sugar
dash hot pepper sauce
1 cup seeded, shredded cucumber
1 cup shredded carrots
3 green onions, with green tops,
    chopped
1/2 cup chopped fresh cilantro

In a large pot of rapidly boiling salted water, cook pasta until slightly firm to the bite, *al dente*, about 8 to 10 minutes. While pasta is cooking, sauté shallots and garlic in 1 tbs. of the canola oil in a nonstick skillet until soft. Add chicken and sauté for 2 to 3 minutes.

In a small bowl, stir together peanut butter, water and sesame oil until blended. Gradually add soy sauce, vinegar, sugar and pepper sauce and stir until smooth. Drain pasta, rinse with cold water and drain again. Transfer to a serving bowl. Add chicken, cucumber, carrots, onions and peanut sauce and toss well. Sprinkle with cilantro. Serve at room temperature or chilled.

FIVE-SPICE CHICKEN AND NOODLE SALAD

Grilled spiced chicken thighs nestle with noodles on a bed of napa cabbage for this tantalizing warm or chilled salad. It makes a lovely luncheon entrée with fresh peaches, nectarines or honeydew melon and candied ginger for dessert. Or you can embellish the salad with fresh fruit slices. Another option is to substitute spinach leaves for the cabbage and carrot slaw.

FIVE-SPICE GINGER SAUCE

1/4 cup seasoned rice vinegar
2 tbs. lemon juice
2 tbs. soy sauce
1 1/2 tbs. dark sesame oil

1 tbs. minced fresh ginger
2 tsp. minced fresh lemon peel (zest)
1 tsp. Chinese five-spice powder

8 oz. dried linguine or fresh Chinese noodles
4 boneless chicken thighs, skin removed if desired
5 cups shredded napa cabbage
2 carrots, shredded
3 green onions, with green tops, chopped
1 bunch fresh cilantro or arugula, chopped

Mix sauce ingredients in a small bowl; set aside.

In a large saucepan, cook pasta or noodles in rapidly boiling salted water until slightly firm to the bite, *al dente,* about 10 minutes for linguine and 2 minutes for fresh noodles. Drain, rinse with cold water to cool and drain again. Place in a large bowl, add ⅔ of the sauce and mix lightly. Set aside.

Heat grill or broiler to high. Brush chicken with remaining sauce and grill or broil for about 5 minutes per side, basting until cooked through. Remove and discard skin if used. Transfer to a board and cut across the grain into strips. Toss together cabbage, carrots, ½ of the onions, and cilantro. Arrange vegetable mixture on each of 4 dinner plates. Spoon noodles onto vegetables and top with chicken. Sprinkle with remaining onions and cilantro.

CASSEROLES AND ONE-DISH MEALS

ASPARAGUS, CHICKEN AND EGGS ITALIAN-STYLE

With fresh asparagus in season, this makes a fast, chic treat for a brunch, luncheon or dinner.

¾ lb. asparagus
2 boneless, skinless chicken breast
    halves, pounded slightly and cut
    into 1-inch strips
1 tbs. butter or oil

2 eggs
salt and freshly ground pepper to taste
1 tsp. chopped fresh tarragon
¼ cup (1 oz.) freshly grated Parmesan
    or Romano cheese

Heat oven to 350°. Trim the ends from asparagus and steam or cook in boiling salted water until tender, about 5 to 7 minutes; drain. In a nonstick skillet, sauté chicken in 1 tsp. of the butter for 2 to 3 minutes, or until browned and almost cooked through. Place remaining butter in two 6-inch ramekins and melt in oven. Break an egg into each ramekin, sprinkle with salt and pepper and bake until whites are barely set, about 6 to 7 minutes. Arrange asparagus and chicken next to eggs, sprinkle with tarragon and cheese and bake until cheese melts and eggs are set, about 2 minutes.

CHICKEN PLATTER DINNER

Servings: 1

Chicken and a quartet of vegetables with an "East meets West" theme make a fast meal when microwaved and served on the same plate. The sweet tang of chutney and hot mustard lends zest. For 2 servings, arrange double the ingredients on 2 plates and cook separately.

1 small yam, peeled and thinly sliced
1 head baby bok choy, or a few Swiss chard leaves, coarsely chopped
1/4 cup chicken stock
1/2 tsp. chopped fresh ginger
2 shiitake mushrooms, stemmed and sliced, or 2 white mushrooms, sliced

8-10 snow pea pods, ends trimmed
1 green onion, with green top, chopped
1 tsp. fresh thyme leaves, or 1/4 tsp. dried
1 boneless, skinless chicken breast half, thinly sliced and fanned slightly
1 tsp. sweet-hot mustard
2 tsp. mango or apricot chutney

On a microwaveable dinner plate, arrange yam near the edge on one side. Arrange bok choy on the opposite outer side. Mix chicken stock and ginger and spoon over vegetables. Cover with vented plastic wrap and cook on HIGH for 5 minutes. Place mushrooms and pea pods in the center of plate and sprinkle with green onion and thyme. Spread chicken with a mixture of mustard and chutney and place over pea pods and mushrooms. Cover with plastic wrap and cook on HIGH for 2 minutes, or until chicken is no longer pink. Let stand for 5 minutes.

POLENTA WITH SUN-DRIED TOMATOES AND CHICKEN

Polenta, a staple of Northern Italy, is really coarse-ground cornmeal. In a pinch, substitute regular cornmeal for very fine results. This is a great make-ahead entrée for brunch, lunch or an informal supper.

1 cup polenta
3½ cups cold water
2 chicken bouillon cubes
salt and freshly ground pepper to taste
2 tbs. extra virgin olive oil
2 tbs. fresh thyme leaves, or 1½ tsp.
   dried

⅓ cup matchstick strips oil-packed
   sun-dried tomatoes
3 cooked chicken thighs, boned and
   cut into strips
½ cup (2 oz.) shredded fontina or
   Jarlsberg cheese
3 tbs. freshly grated Parmesan cheese

Soak polenta in 1½ cups of the water for 10 minutes. In a large saucepan, bring remaining 2 cups water and bouillon cubes to a boil and stir in soaked polenta. Bring back to a boil, reduce heat to low and simmer, stirring occasionally, for 15 minutes. Stir in salt, pepper, oil and thyme. Pour into a greased 9-inch pie pan. Cool mixture if making ahead of time. Heat oven to 300°. Top polenta with tomatoes, chicken and cheeses. Bake for 15 minutes or 25 minutes if chilled, or until heated through. Cut into wedges to serve.

CHICKEN RISOTTO WITH MUSHROOMS

Servings: 4

This is a soul-satisfying dish for an informal dinner. Italian short-grain arborio rice is a must for achieving the proper texture. For the best flavor, use homemade chicken stock.

2½-3 cups chicken stock
1½ tbs. unsalted butter
1½ tbs. olive oil
⅓ cup chopped white sweet onion
1 cup arborio rice
1 tsp. grated fresh lemon peel (zest)
2 boneless, skinless chicken breast halves, cut into ½-inch strips
¼ lb. white mushrooms, sliced
salt and freshly ground pepper to taste
¼ cup (1 oz.) freshly grated Parmesan or Romano cheese
2 tbs. chopped fresh flat-leaf parsley

In a medium saucepan, bring chicken stock to a boil; reduce heat to low and keep stock at a simmer. In a medium saucepan, heat 1 tbs. of the butter and 1 tbs. of the oil over medium-low heat. Add onion and cook for about 2 to 3 minutes, until translucent. Add rice and cook, stirring, for about 3 minutes, until center turns opaque. Add ½ cup of the hot stock and lemon peel and cook, stirring constantly, until stock is absorbed. Add another ½ cup of the stock, and cook, stirring, until stock is absorbed. Repeat process, adding ½ cup stock twice more, until absorbed. Add additional stock as needed until rice is slightly firm to the bite in the center, *al dente*, and creamy on the outside.

While rice is cooking, sauté chicken and mushrooms in remaining butter for 2 to 3 minutes, or until just cooked through; add to cooked risotto. Season with salt and pepper and sprinkle with cheese and parsley.

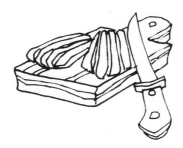

CHICKEN AND APRICOT TAJINE

Servings: 4

Honey, lime, pistachios and a melange of spices provide delicious Moroccan overtones for nuggets of dark-meat chicken.

1 small onion, chopped
1 tsp. minced fresh ginger
1 stick cinnamon
$\frac{1}{8}$ tsp. ground turmeric
$\frac{1}{8}$ tsp. ground coriander
1 tsp. olive oil
1 clove garlic, minced
5 boneless, skinless chicken thighs, cut into $1\frac{1}{4}$-inch cubes

salt and freshly ground pepper to taste
12 dried apricot halves
1 tbs. honey
$1\frac{1}{2}$ tbs. lime or lemon juice
2 tbs. chopped pistachio nuts or pine nuts
cilantro or flat-leaf parsley sprigs for garnish
lime or lemon wedges for garnish

Heat oven to 350°. In a heavy ovenproof saucepan or Dutch oven, sauté onion, ginger, cinnamon, turmeric and coriander in oil for about 2 minutes, until softened. Add garlic, chicken, salt and pepper and sauté until browned, about 10 minutes. Cover and bake for 20 minutes. Remove from oven and add apricot halves, honey and lime juice to pan drippings and bake for 10 additional minutes, or until cooked through. To serve, sprinkle with nuts and garnish with cilantro sprigs and lime wedges.

CHICKEN TAMALE PIE

Fresh white corn lends a wonderful sweet crunch to this old-time favorite.

2 cups chicken stock
1/2 cup cornmeal
1/4 cup chopped onion
1 clove garlic, minced
1 tbs. olive oil
2 Roma tomatoes, peeled and chopped
1/4 tsp. dried oregano
1/4 tsp. dried thyme
chili powder to taste

kernels from 3 ears fresh white corn, or
    1 1/2 cups frozen corn
salt and freshly ground pepper to taste
2 cups cooked shredded chicken,
    preferably dark meat
1/2 cup (2 oz.) shredded sharp cheddar
    cheese
2 tbs. chopped fresh oregano or flat-
    leaf parsley for garnish

Stir 1/2 cup of the stock into cornmeal and let stand for 10 minutes. In a saucepan, bring remaining stock to a boil, stir in cornmeal, reduce heat to low, cover and cook for 10 to 15 minutes, or until mixture thickens. Cool slightly and use to line the bottom and sides of a greased 2-quart casserole. Heat oven to 375°. In a large skillet over medium heat, sauté onion and garlic in oil until translucent. Stir in tomatoes, oregano, thyme and chili powder and cook for 15 minutes. Add corn, salt and pepper. Spread chicken in cornmeal-lined casserole and cover with tomato-corn mixture. Sprinkle with cheese and bake for 25 minutes, or until heated through. Garnish with oregano.

CHICKEN INDIENNE

For a party buffet, accent this Indian-style chicken with an orange and chutney glaze with a wreath of fresh fruit. Instead of using quartered chickens, you can prepare it with 8 split breasts or attached drumsticks and thighs if desired.

2 broiler-fryers, about 3-3½ lb. each,
    quartered
salt and freshly ground pepper to taste
1⅓ cups orange juice
⅓ cup mango chutney
½ tsp. cinnamon
½ tsp. ground ginger

1 tsp. curry powder
½ cup chicken stock
½ cup golden raisins *(half chopped dried apricots*
⅓ cup toasted slivered almonds
sliced fresh fruit: mango, oranges, kiwi
    fruit and/or seedless grapes

Heat oven to 425°. Arrange chicken in a greased shallow baking dish. Season with salt and pepper. Bake for 20 minutes, or until golden brown. While chicken is baking, combine orange juice, chutney, cinnamon, ginger, curry powder, chicken stock and raisins in a saucepan. Simmer uncovered until slightly thickened. Pour sauce over browned chicken, reduce oven heat to 375° and bake for 20 minutes, or until chicken is cooked through, basting frequently. Arrange chicken on a platter, sprinkle with nuts and garnish with a garland of fruit.

NOTE: Breasts may be done 5 to 10 minutes before legs.

GREEK CHICKEN STIFATHO

Traditionally, a fryer is used for this classic dish. For neat portions, use all thighs instead and remove the skin to streamline the fat.

1 tsp. olive oil
1 medium onion, chopped
2 cloves garlic, minced
1 broiler-fryer, about 3-3½ lb., cut into portions, or 8 chicken thighs
1 cup richly flavored low-fat chicken stock
½ cup tomato paste

3 tbs. red wine vinegar
1½ tsp. mixed pickling spice, tied in cheesecloth
salt and freshly ground pepper to taste
12 small red potatoes, halved
½ lb. small boiling onions, peeled, root end slashed in a cross
2 tbs. minced fresh flat-leaf parsley

In a large saucepan over medium heat, heat oil and sauté onion for about 2 to 3 minutes, until soft. Add garlic and chicken and cook for about 4 to 5 minutes per side, until browned. Add stock, tomato paste, vinegar and pickling spice. Season with salt and pepper. Cover and simmer for 15 minutes. Add potatoes and onions and simmer for 20 to 25 minutes, or until chicken and vegetables are cooked through. Skim any fat from the surface of cooking liquid and remove pickling spices. Serve garnished with parsley.

NOTE: Breast may be done 5 to 10 minutes before legs.

COQ AU VIN

This classic French dish calls for an accompaniment of steamed white and wild rice. Crostini with mushrooms and chevre or Roquefort would be a luxurious starter. If you can't find small mushrooms, use larger ones and cut them in half.

4 chicken breast halves
4 chicken drumsticks
2 chicken thighs
2 tsp. olive oil
2 tsp. butter
½ lb. pearl onions, peeled
1 tsp. brown sugar
1 cup dry red wine
¾ cup richly flavored low-fat chicken stock
salt and freshly ground pepper to taste
2 cloves garlic, minced
2 tsp. chopped fresh rosemary, or ½ tsp. dried
1 tbs. cornstarch blended with 1 tbs. cold water
½ lb. small white mushrooms

Heat oven to 350°. In a large skillet over medium-high heat, brown chicken parts in 1 tsp. of the oil and 1 tsp. of the butter for about 10 minutes, turning to brown all sides. Transfer to a large ovenproof casserole. Add onions to pan and brown with sugar until slightly caramelized; add to casserole with chicken. Pour wine and stock into pan and bring to a boil, scraping up browned bits; reduce slightly. Pour wine mixture over chicken and season with salt, pepper, garlic and rosemary. Cover and bake for 25 minutes, or until chicken is barely tender. Mix cornstarch paste in a small saucepan and pour in wine juices from casserole. Stir thickened wine juices into casserole with chicken. Sauté mushrooms in remaining oil and butter and add to casserole. Continue to bake chicken until tender, about 15 minutes longer.

NOTE: Breasts may be done 5 to 10 minutes before legs.

CHICKEN TUSCANY-STYLE

Plump stuffed mushrooms accompany wine-enhanced chicken breasts for this sumptuous entrée. It is ideal to assemble in advance to bake later for guests.

16 white mushrooms, about 1¾ inches in diameter
1 tbs. butter
⅓ cup chopped onion
¼ lb. ground veal or chicken
¼ tsp. salt
freshly ground pepper to taste
1 tbs. minced fresh sage or oregano, or ¾ tsp. dried
⅓ cup (1⅓ oz.) freshly grated Parmesan cheese
¼ cup chopped prosciutto or ham
2 tbs. dry breadcrumbs

8 boneless, skinless chicken breast halves
salt and freshly ground pepper to taste
1 tbs. butter
1 tbs. olive oil
½ cup chopped onion
1 large tomato, peeled and diced
½ cup chicken stock
½ cup dry white wine
¼ cup minced prosciutto or Black Forest ham
2 tbs. chopped fresh basil for garnish
2 tbs. chopped fresh flat-leaf parsley for garnish

Remove stems of mushrooms and chop stems finely. Cook chopped stems in 1 tbs. butter with ⅓ cup chopped onion until vegetables are soft. Add ground veal, ¼ tsp. salt and pepper and cook for a few minutes longer. Mix in sage, Parmesan cheese, ¼ cup prosciutto and breadcrumbs. Pack filling into mushroom caps; set aside.

Season chicken with salt and pepper. In a large skillet, brown chicken in 1 tbs. butter and oil for about 10 minutes, turning to brown both sides. Transfer to a casserole. In skillet, brown stuffed mushrooms and transfer to casserole with chicken. Add ½ cup chopped onion and tomato to skillet and sauté until onion is soft. Add stock and wine and cook rapidly until liquid is reduced by half. Stir in ¼ cup prosciutto and spoon mixture over chicken in casserole. If desired, cover and chill. Bring to room temperature before baking.

Heat oven to 400°. Bake casserole for 20 minutes, or until cooked through. Sprinkle with basil and parsley.

CHICKEN WITH LENTILS AND ORANGES

Servings: 4-6

For a potluck, chicken thighs in an orange glaze, nestled on a bed of lentils, makes a welcome dish. Ring it with orange segments and basil for a pretty presentation.

3 cups water
1¼ cups lentils
salt and freshly ground pepper to taste
2 cloves garlic, minced
2 shallots, chopped
2 tbs. red wine vinegar
2 tbs. roasted garlic-flavored tomato
    paste

6 boneless, skinless chicken thighs
1 tsp. olive oil
salt and freshly ground pepper to taste
⅓ cup orange juice
2 tbs. balsamic vinegar
2 oranges or tangerines, cut into
    sections or sliced, for garnish
chopped fresh basil for garnish

In a large saucepan, bring water to a boil. Reduce heat to low, add lentils, salt, pepper, garlic and shallots; simmer for 15 minutes. Add wine vinegar and tomato paste and cook for 10 minutes longer, until slightly firm to the bite, *al dente*. In a large skillet over medium-high heat, sauté chicken in oil for 10 minutes, turning to brown both sides. Season with salt and pepper. Add orange juice and balsamic vinegar and simmer for 5 minutes longer, or until cooked through. Add to lentils the last few minutes of cooking. Garnish with orange sections and chopped basil.

SAUTÉS AND STIR-FRIES

CHICKEN BREASTS WITH ROSEMARY AND RASPBERRY VINEGAR

Servings: 2

This is a superb way to cook lean chicken breasts. Pounding them slightly with a round metal mallet makes them cook evenly and fast. The interplay of rosemary, shallots and tangy berry juices enhances this chicken cutlet. If fresh raspberries are available, they make a juicy, mouth-filling finish.

2 boneless, skinless chicken breast halves
1 tbs. butter or olive oil
1 shallot, chopped
1 clove garlic, minced
2 tsp. chopped fresh rosemary, or
⅓ tsp. dried

salt and freshly ground pepper to taste
⅓ cup richly flavored chicken stock
3 tbs. raspberry vinegar
1 tbs. cassis (black currant) syrup
½ cup raspberries or blueberries for
garnish, optional

Place chicken between 2 sheets of plastic wrap and pound lightly with a mallet to an even thickness. In a large nonstick skillet over medium heat, heat butter and sauté shallot, garlic and rosemary for 2 minutes. Season chicken with salt and pepper and sauté for about 3 to 4 minutes, turning once, or until just cooked through. Remove chicken from pan, add stock and cook until liquid is reduced by half. Add vinegar and cassis and reduce until syrupy. Return chicken to pan and heat through in sauce. Transfer to warm serving plates and scatter berries over the top, if desired.

CHICKEN WITH CAPERS AND LEMON

Servings: 2

This piquant entrée begs for linguine or tagliarini as a sidekick and olive oil-glazed zucchini or yellow summer squash. An Italian tri-color salad of sliced tomatoes, mozzarella cheese and fresh basil might commence the meal. Lemon or coffee gelato might follow for dessert.

2 boneless, skinless chicken breast
   halves
1 tbs. olive oil
1 shallot, chopped
1 clove garlic, minced
salt and freshly ground pepper to taste

¼ cup richly-flavored chicken stock
2 tbs. lemon juice
2 tsp. capers, rinsed
2 rolled anchovy fillets for garnish
1 tbs. minced fresh chives for garnish

Place chicken between 2 sheets of plastic wrap and pound lightly with a mallet to an even thickness. In a large nonstick skillet over medium heat, heat oil and sauté shallot and garlic for 2 minutes. Season chicken with salt and pepper and sauté for 3 to 4 minutes, turning once, or until just cooked through. Transfer to warm serving plates. Add chicken stock, lemon juice and capers to skillet and cook until liquid is slightly reduced. Spoon sauce over chicken and garnish with anchovy fillets and chives.

SIZZLING CHICKEN SOSTANZA

A popular trattoria in Florence named Sostanza set forth this simple chicken dish for a succulent repast with fresh asparagus on one of my early trips to Italy.

4 boneless, skinless chicken breast halves
flour seasoned with salt and pepper
3 tbs. unsalted butter
1/3 lb. small white mushrooms, halved
2 tbs. lemon juice
chopped fresh chives for garnish
lemon wedges for garnish

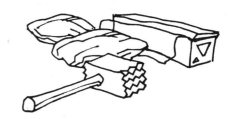

Place chicken between 2 sheets of plastic wrap and pound lightly with a mallet to an even thickness. Coat chicken lightly with seasoned flour and shake off excess. In a large skillet over medium heat, heat butter and sauté chicken for 3 to 4 minutes, turning once, or until just cooked through. Transfer to warm serving plates. Add mushrooms and lemon juice to skillet and sauté for about 1 minute. Spoon mushrooms and pan juices over chicken. Sprinkle with chives and garnish with lemon wedges.

CHICKEN BREASTS WITH SPINACH AND MUSHROOMS

Crispy crumb-coated chicken breasts rest on a bed of spinach with a butter-sautéed mushroom topping for a delicious combination.

2 boneless, skinless chicken breast
   halves
1/4 cup seasoned fine dry sourdough
   breadcrumbs
2 tbs. butter or olive oil
1 lb. spinach, stemmed

salt and freshly ground pepper to taste
1/4 lb. white mushrooms, sliced
1 tbs. minced fresh chives for garnish
1 tbs. minced fresh flat-leaf parsley for
   garnish

Place chicken between 2 sheets of plastic wrap and pound lightly with a mallet to an even thickness. Turn chicken in crumbs to coat lightly. In a large nonstick skillet over medium heat, heat 1 tbs. of the butter and sauté chicken for 3 to 4 minutes, turning once, or until just cooked through. Remove from pan and keep warm. Steam spinach just until wilted, season with salt and pepper and transfer to warm serving plates; arrange chicken on top of spinach. Sauté mushrooms in remaining butter or oil until softened, about 2 minutes, and spoon over chicken. Garnish with chives and parsley.

CHICKEN WITH SUN-DRIED TOMATOES AND OLIVES

Succulent sun-dried tomatoes and piquant black olives embellish this fast chicken sauté. Chicken thighs work nicely in this dish in place of breasts; in this case, extend the cooking time a few minutes and use red wine instead of white.

4 boneless, skinless chicken breast halves, or 6 boneless, skinless chicken thighs
1 tbs. olive oil
1 large onion, chopped
4 cloves garlic, minced
salt and freshly ground pepper to taste
¾ cup dry white wine or red wine
½ lemon, thinly sliced and seeded
12 Mediterranean-style black olives, pitted
⅓ cup matchstick strips oil-packed sun-dried tomatoes
2 tbs. slivered fresh basil leaves
fresh basil sprigs for garnish

Place chicken between 2 sheets of plastic wrap and pound lightly with a mallet to an even thickness. In a large skillet over medium heat, heat oil and sauté onion and garlic until soft. Season chicken with salt and pepper and sauté for 2 to 3 minutes, turning once, or until almost cooked through. Remove from skillet and keep warm. Add wine to skillet and simmer for 2 minutes. Return chicken to pan and add lemon slices, olives and tomatoes. Cover and cook for 2 to 3 minutes longer, or until cooked through. Transfer chicken to warm serving plates. Reduce cooking liquid until syrupy and spoon over chicken, dividing olives, tomatoes and lemon slices evenly. Sprinkle with slivered basil and garnish with basil sprigs.

CHICKEN AND MUSHROOMS PIQUANT

Servings: 4

Using French seasonings instead of Oriental ones, here is a quick stir-fry with chicken breast strips and mushrooms.

240   2 tbs. olive oil
1 shallot, finely chopped
1 clove garlic, minced
40   1/3 lb. white mushrooms, thinly sliced
870   3 boneless, skinless chicken breast
     halves, cut into 3/8-inch strips
30   1 tbs. cornstarch
salt and freshly ground pepper to taste

25   1/3 cup dry white wine
16   1/3 cup chicken stock
10   2 tsp. Dijon mustard
1/2 tsp. anchovy paste
1 tbs. minced fresh parsley for garnish
1 tbs. minced fresh chives or green
     onion tops for garnish

+/1225
305

Heat a large nonstick skillet or wok over medium heat, add 1 tbs. of the oil and stir-fry shallot, garlic and mushrooms for 2 minutes, just until heated through; transfer to a platter. Dip chicken pieces in a mixture of cornstarch, salt and pepper, shake off excess and stir-fry in remaining oil, just until browned on both sides. Pour wine and stock into pan and stir-fry for about 3 minutes, until chicken is cooked through and liquid is reduced by half. Stir in mustard and anchovy paste. Return mushroom mixture to pan and heat through. Spoon onto plates and garnish with parsley and chives.

CASHEW CHICKEN

Assemble the ingredients on the counter before cooking this multi-textured Asian dish. Jicama provides a fresh, interesting crunch along with the cashews.

3 boneless, skinless chicken breast halves
1/2 tsp. cornstarch
1/2 cup cashew nuts
2 tbs. peanut or canola oil
1/2 cup chicken stock
1/4 lb. white mushrooms, sliced
3/4 cup thinly sliced jicama or bamboo shoots (1/2-x-1-inch slices)

1 1/2 cups snow pea pods, ends trimmed and strings removed
dash ground white pepper
2 tsp. light soy sauce
few drops sesame oil
1 1/2 tsp. cornstarch dissolved in 1 tbs. cold water
hot steamed rice

Cut chicken horizontally into wafer-thin slices. Cut slices into 1 1/2-inch squares. Toss chicken lightly in cornstarch and shake off excess. In a large skillet or wok over medium heat, stir-fry nuts in 1 tsp. of the oil until lightly browned; transfer to a plate and keep warm. Heat remaining oil, add chicken and stir-fry over high heat for 1 minute, or until chicken turns white. Add stock, mushrooms, jicama and pea pods. Cover pan and cook for 1 1/2 minutes. Remove lid and add pepper, soy sauce, sesame oil and cornstarch mixture. Cook, stirring, until sauce is thickened. Serve with rice.

STIR-FRIED ASPARAGUS AND CHICKEN WITH BLACK BEANS

Servings: 2-3

When spring brings fresh asparagus season, this is a superb way to savor it with chicken and Oriental seasonings. Salted, fermented black beans are a staple Chinese ingredient in Oriental markets. If kept in the freezer, they have a long storage life.

¾ lb. asparagus, cut into 1-inch diagonal slices
1 tbs. fermented black beans
2 cloves garlic, minced
1 tbs. minced fresh ginger
2 boneless, skinless chicken breast halves
cornstarch
2 tbs. peanut or vegetable oil
2 green onions, with half of the green tops, chopped
½ cup low-salt chicken stock
1 tbs. light soy sauce
½ tsp. dark sesame oil
2 tsp. cornstarch
1 tbs. water
1 tsp. oyster sauce, optional
hot steamed rice

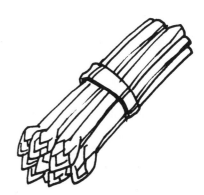

Cook asparagus in boiling water for 1 minute. Drain and cool under cold running water; set aside.

In a small bowl, cover black beans with warm water and soak for 1 minute. Drain and rinse thoroughly to remove salt. Place beans in a bowl with garlic and ginger; mash into a paste and set aside.

Cut chicken into ¾-inch strips and coat with cornstarch, shaking off excess. Heat a wok or large skillet over medium-high heat, add 1 tbs. of the oil, add chicken and stir-fry for 2 minutes. Transfer to a plate. Add remaining oil to hot pan, add black bean paste and stir-fry until fragrant, a few seconds. Toss in onions and stir-fry for 10 seconds. Add asparagus to pan in 2 or 3 batches, seconds apart, making certain the wok is hot before adding more. Pour in stock, soy sauce and sesame oil and bring to a boil. If asparagus needs more cooking, cover wok and cook for 1 minute. Stir together cornstarch, water and oyster sauce, if using, to make a smooth paste. When asparagus is crisp-tender, add cornstarch paste to the center of wok and stir until sauce is thickened. Return chicken to pan and stir. Serve with rice.

MILANESE CHICKEN AND ARTICHOKES

Servings: 4

This flavor-packed chicken dish using pounded chicken breasts is a refined update on the Italian classic recipe, which is usually done with chicken parts.

4 boneless, skinless chicken breast
   halves
salt and freshly ground pepper to taste
½ tsp. dried tarragon
1 tbs. olive oil
1 tbs. butter
¼ lb. small white mushrooms

1½ tbs. lemon juice
⅓ cup dry vermouth or white wine
1 tbs. dry sherry
1 pkg. (8 oz.) frozen artichoke hearts,
   cooked, or 8 oz. fresh artichoke
   hearts, cooked

Place chicken between 2 sheets of plastic wrap and pound lightly with a mallet to an even thickness. Season chicken with salt, pepper and tarragon. In a large skillet over medium heat, heat oil and butter and sauté chicken, turning once, for 3 to 4 minutes, or until just cooked through. Transfer to a warm platter. Add mushrooms to pan with the lemon juice, vermouth and sherry and simmer for 2 minutes. Add artichokes and cook until heated through. Spoon over chicken.

CHICKEN WITH MUSTARD AND GRUYÈRE

Servings: 2

A fast broil gives a golden finish to these cheese-crusted chicken breasts.

2 boneless, skinless chicken breast
   halves
1 tbs. butter or olive oil
1 shallot, chopped
1 clove garlic, minced
salt and freshly ground pepper to taste

1/4 cup richly-flavored chicken stock
3 tbs. heavy cream
1 1/2 tbs. Dijon mustard
1/3 cup (1 1/3 oz.) shredded Gruyère or
   Jarlsberg cheese
1 tbs. minced fresh chives for garnish

Place chicken between 2 sheets of plastic wrap and pound lightly with a mallet to an even thickness. In a large nonstick skillet over medium heat, heat butter or oil and sauté shallot and garlic for 2 minutes, until softened. Season chicken with salt and pepper and sauté for about 2 to 3 minutes, turning once, or until almost cooked through. Transfer to an ovenproof serving dish. Heat broiler. Add stock, cream and mustard to pan juices, bring to a boil and reduce liquid slightly. Add 1/2 of the cheese to sauce and spoon over chicken. Sprinkle with remaining cheese and broil until cheese is melted, about 1 minute. Sprinkle with chives.

CHICKEN VERONIQUE

Seedless green or red grapes explode with sweet fruitiness in this fast sauté.

2 boneless, skinless chicken breast halves
1 tsp. butter
1 tsp. olive oil
1½ tsp. orange marmalade
2 tsp. chopped fresh tarragon, or ½ tsp. dried
salt and freshly ground pepper to taste
¼ cup dry white wine
2 tbs. heavy cream
1 tsp. cornstarch mixed with 1 tsp. water
⅔ cup seedless red or green grapes

Place chicken between 2 sheets of plastic wrap and pound lightly with a mallet to an even thickness. In a large skillet over medium heat, heat butter and oil and sauté chicken for about 3 to 4 minutes, turning once, or until just cooked through. Transfer to a warm platter or serving plates. Add marmalade, tarragon, salt, pepper and wine and cook until liquid is slightly reduced. Stir in cream and heat through. Stir in cornstarch-water mixture, bring to a boil and stir until thickened. Mix in grapes and pour over chicken.

CHICKEN BREASTS WITH PORT AND CHERRIES

Nuggets of tangy-sweet dried cherries embellish this wine-laced entrée. I like to accompany it with white and wild rice and butter-tossed steamed sugar snap peas or fresh asparagus.

2 boneless, skinless chicken breast
   halves
1 tbs. butter or olive oil
1 shallot, minced
1 clove garlic, minced

salt and freshly ground pepper to taste
1/3 cup chicken stock
2 tbs. port
2 tbs. heavy cream
2 tbs. dried cherries

Place chicken between 2 sheets of plastic wrap and pound lightly with a mallet to an even thickness. In a large nonstick skillet over medium heat, heat butter or oil and sauté shallot and garlic for 2 to 3 minutes, until softened. Season chicken with salt and pepper and sauté for about 3 to 4 minutes, turning once, or until just cooked through. Transfer chicken to a plate. Add chicken stock to pan and cook until liquid is reduced slightly. Add port and cream and reduce until syrupy. Return chicken to pan and heat through in sauce. Transfer to warm serving plates and scatter cherries over the top.

CHICKEN SCALOPPINE-STYLE WITH BRANDY

This makes a perfect company entrée with a partner of couscous or tagliarini and steamed tiny green beans or broccoli florets. A spinach salad dressed with strawberries, pistachios and feta cheese, or with winter pears, toasted hazelnuts and Gorgonzola, makes a choice starter. Ideally, use a richly flavored chicken stock to add flavor.

2 boneless, skinless chicken breast
   halves
1 tbs. butter or olive oil
1 shallot, chopped
1 clove garlic, minced

salt and freshly ground pepper to taste
1/4 cup richly-flavored chicken stock
2 tbs. brandy
2 tbs. heavy cream
1 tbs. minced fresh chives for garnish

Place chicken between 2 sheets of plastic wrap and pound lightly with a mallet to an even thickness. In a large nonstick skillet over medium heat, heat butter and sauté shallot and garlic for 2 to 3 minutes, until softened. Season chicken with salt and pepper and sauté for about 3 to 4 minutes, turning once, or until just cooked through. Transfer chicken to a plate. Add chicken stock to pan and cook until reduced by half. Add brandy and cream and reduce until syrupy. Return chicken to pan and heat through in sauce. Divide among warm serving plates and garnish with chives.

BRANDIED CHICKEN WITH MUSHROOMS

This is a fast, elegant guest dish when you feel like splurging with a little cream in the menu.

4 boneless, skinless chicken breast
   halves
salt and freshly ground pepper to taste
1 shallot, chopped
1 clove garlic, minced
1/8 tsp. nutmeg
2 tbs. olive oil

2 tbs. butter
1/2 lb. small white mushrooms
3/4 cup heavy cream
1 1/2 tbs. brandy or cognac
1 1/2 tbs. dry sherry
hot cooked white and wild rice

Place chicken between 2 sheets of plastic wrap and pound lightly with a mallet to an even thickness. Season chicken with salt, pepper, shallots, garlic and nutmeg. In a large nonstick skillet over medium heat, sauté chicken breasts in 1 tbs. each of the oil and butter until browned and cooked through, about 3 to 4 minutes. Transfer to a warm platter. Sauté mushrooms in remaining oil and butter, for about 2 minutes, just until softened. Add cream, brandy and sherry to pan and cook down slightly. Spoon rice onto plates with chicken and spoon mushroom sauce over the top.

FRENCH COUNTRY CHICKEN IN WINE CREAM

Servings: 4

This simple country French-style dish goes nicely with a bundle of fresh aspara-gus or stack of tiny green beans. I like to finish off with raspberry sorbet or strawberries splashed with cassis (black currant) syrup over vanilla bean ice cream.

4 boneless, skinless chicken breast
    halves
salt and freshly ground pepper to taste
1 tsp. butter or olive oil
1 shallot, minced
2 cloves garlic, minced
3 tbs. dry white wine

3 tbs. white wine vinegar
1 medium tomato, peeled and diced
2 tsp. chopped fresh tarragon, or
    1/2 tsp. dried, crushed
1/3 cup heavy cream
1 tbs. chopped fresh chives or flat-leaf
    parsley

Place chicken between 2 sheets of plastic wrap and pound lightly with a mallet to an even thickness. Season chicken breasts with salt and pepper. In a large skillet over medium heat, sauté chicken in butter or oil, turning to brown both sides. Add shallot, garlic and wine to pan. Cover and simmer for 8 to 10 minutes, or until just cooked through. Transfer chicken to a warm platter, pour off pan juices and reserve. Pour vinegar into pan and cook until reduced by half. Add tomato and tarragon and cook until heated through. Pour in cream and reserved pan juices, stir and cook until liquid is slightly reduced. Spoon sauce over chicken and sprinkle with chives or parsley.

CHICKEN NORMANDY

A trio of apple flavors — cider, Calvados and sautéed apple slices — enhances this chicken entrée. If Calvados (apple brandy) is missing from your cupboard, substitute brandy or cognac.

4 boneless, skinless chicken breast halves
1 tsp. butter
1 tsp. oil
3 tbs. Calvados or brandy, warmed
1 small white onion, minced
1/4 tsp. dried thyme

salt and freshly ground pepper to taste
1/3 cup apple cider or apple juice
2 tart apples, peeled, cored and sliced
1 tbs. butter
1 tbs. sugar
1/3 cup heavy cream

Place chicken between 2 sheets of plastic wrap and pound lightly with a mallet to an even thickness. In a large skillet over medium heat, heat 1 tsp. butter and oil and sauté chicken for about 3 to 4 minutes, turning once, or until just cooked through. Add Calvados and carefully ignite with a match away from the heat. When flame subsides, return pan to heat and add onion, thyme, salt, pepper and cider. Cover and simmer for 4 to 5 minutes, or until cooked through. Sauté apples in 1 tbs. butter and sugar until tender and caramelized. Transfer chicken to a warm platter and place apple slices alongside. Stir cream into pan juices and heat until liquid is reduced slightly. Pour some of the sauce over chicken and pass remainder at the table.

CHICKEN THIGHS AND MANGOES MARRAKESH

Good

Aromatic chicken thighs are refreshed with juicy mango slices in this festive entrée.

1 small onion, chopped
2 tsp. minced fresh ginger
1 tsp. ground cumin
½ tsp. ground allspice
1 small stick cinnamon – don't crush
1 T, ~~½ tsp.~~ olive oil   120
2 cloves garlic, minced

on bone in
4 - 6 boneless, skinless chicken thighs   750
salt and freshly ground pepper to taste
1 tbs. honey   100
2 tbs. lime or lemon juice
1 mango
1 lime, cut into wedges, for garnish   65
2T raisens   90
2T almonds (skip)

In a large skillet over medium heat, sauté onion, ginger, cumin, allspice and cinnamon in oil until onion is softened. Add garlic, chicken, salt and pepper and brown lightly on all sides. Cover and cook over low heat for 15 to 20 minutes, or until cooked through. Stir in honey and lime juice and turn chicken in sauce. Spoon onto warm serving plates. Peel and slice mango and arrange 2 or 3 slices on each serving plate. Garnish with lime wedges for squeezing over individual servings.

10 05
120
3 | 1125

with almonds serving   375
w/o almonds 1 serving   345

Good!

CHICKEN THIGHS WITH
BALSAMIC ORANGE SAUCE

Often the simplest is best, as with this fast fresh orange juice and balsamic vinegar sauce for chicken thighs. If any gelatinized chicken juices are left from roasting a chicken, they make a superb addition.

or bone in

4 boneless, skinless chicken thighs
salt and freshly ground pepper to taste
1/4 tsp. dried tarragon
1 tbs. fruity olive oil
3/4 cup orange juice

2 tbs. balsamic vinegar
2 tbs. gelatinized chicken juices, or
    1/4 cup chicken stock, optional
arugula leaves or watercress for garnish

Place chicken between 2 sheets of plastic wrap and pound lightly with a mallet to an even thickness. Season chicken with salt, pepper and tarragon. In a large skillet, heat oil and sauté chicken, turning to brown both sides. Cover and cook on medium-low for 3 to 4 minutes. Add orange juice and simmer for 5 to 7 minutes longer, or until chicken is cooked through. Transfer chicken to a warm serving platter and keep warm. Reduce orange juice by half, add vinegar and chicken juices, if desired, and reduce until syrupy. Spoon sauce over chicken and garnish with arugula or watercress.

Chicken would probably work fine with "bone in" — just would need more cooking time.

DANISH CHICKEN HASH

Servings: 2

Leftover chicken and spuds reappear as delicious comfort food in this colorful combination.

2 tbs. olive oil
1 small red onion, thinly sliced
2 medium potatoes, preferably Yukon gold, boiled or steamed, peeled and sliced
¼ lb. white mushrooms, sliced
1 large cooked boneless, skinless chicken breast half, diced
3 oz. thinly sliced ham, diced
salt and freshly ground pepper to taste
2 eggs
1 cup cherry tomatoes, halved
chopped chives or green onion tops for garnish

In a large skillet over medium heat, heat oil and sauté onion for about 2 to 3 minutes, until soft. Add potatoes and cook until crusty, turning occasionally. Add mushrooms, chicken and ham and heat through. Season with salt and pepper. Make 2 wells in hash and break eggs into cavities. Ring with cherry tomatoes. Cover and cook until eggs are cooked as desired. Garnish with chives or onions.

MANDARIN ROLLED CHICKEN PANCAKES

Servings: 4

With barbecued chicken on hand, this impromptu Chinese supper can go together instantly. A basket of Oriental vegetables — jicama, sugar snap peas, daikon and Chinese cabbage — provides an edible centerpiece to serve with sea salt and soy sauce for dipping alongside. Sliced tangerines or plums in season are a light finale.

eight 6-inch flour tortillas
3 cups cooked chicken strips
2 tbs. canola oil
1 tbs. light soy sauce

1 bunch green onions, chopped
1 bunch cilantro
hoisin sauce

Place tortillas, 2 at a time, in a hot, ungreased skillet. Heat for 30 seconds, turn over and heat for 30 seconds longer. Remove from skillet and keep warm in a towel. Or, wrap tortillas in aluminum foil and place in a heated 350° oven for 10 minutes.

In a large skillet over medium heat, sauté chicken in oil with soy sauce for about 2 minutes, or just until heated through. Place hot chicken, onions, cilantro and hoisin sauce in separate dishes. Let guests fill and roll their own pancakes at the table.

MU SHU CHICKEN

This last-minute Asian stir-fry makes a convivial family-style entrée to tuck into flour tortillas.

twelve 6-inch flour tortillas
2 green onions
1 tbs. canola oil
1 tsp. sesame oil
2 boneless, skinless chicken breast halves,
    cut into $\frac{1}{8}$-inch-thick strips
$\frac{1}{3}$ cup chopped white onion
1 tsp. minced fresh ginger
1 clove garlic, minced
$\frac{1}{4}$ lb. white mushrooms, sliced
$\frac{1}{2}$ cup sliced jicama
2 stalks fennel, thinly sliced (about $\frac{1}{2}$ cup)
2 tsp. light soy sauce
$\frac{1}{2}$ tsp. brown sugar
3 eggs, lightly beaten

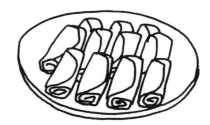

Heat oven to 350°. Wrap tortillas in aluminum foil and heat in oven for 10 minutes.

Chop white parts of onions. Cut green tops into 1½-inch lengths. Make several ¼-inch slashes in one end of each green onion top and place in a bowl of ice water; let stand for 5 to 10 minutes to fan out.

Heat 2 tsp. of the canola oil and 1 tsp. sesame oil in a large skillet. Add chicken, chopped white onion and ginger and stir-fry for 2 minutes. Add garlic, mushrooms, jicama and fennel and stir-fry for 1 minute. Add soy sauce and sugar and heat, stirring, until blended. In a small skillet, heat remaining 1 tsp. canola oil. Pour in beaten eggs and cook, stirring, until barely set. Spoon scrambled eggs onto a platter, cover with chicken-mushroom mixture and surround with onion fans. Let guests fill and roll their own pancakes at the table.

NOTE: If desired, substitute 3 dried shiitake mushrooms for button mushrooms. Place shiitakes in a small bowl, cover with water and let stand for 15 minutes. Drain, chop coarsely and cook with chicken.

GRILLS AND BROILS

CHICKEN SPIEDINI

The skewers can be assembled in advance and refrigerated, ready for cooking at the last minute for company. If desired, brush sliced crusty country bread with garlic oil, grill at the last minute and serve as an accompaniment.

4 boneless, skinless chicken breast halves
2 tbs. Dijon mustard
2 oz. prosciutto, very thinly sliced
2 oz. fontina, Gruyère or Jarlsberg cheese
2 tbs. chopped fresh flat-leaf parsley

1 tbs. chopped fresh oregano, or ¾ tsp. dried
2 tsp. olive oil
1½ tbs. lemon juice
1 clove garlic, minced
freshly ground pepper to taste

Heat broiler. Place chicken between 2 sheets of plastic wrap and pound very thinly with a mallet; cut into 12 rectangles. Lay chicken pieces flat on a board and spread lightly with mustard. Cut prosciutto and cheese into 12 pieces each and lay 1 slice of each on top of chicken strips. Sprinkle with parsley and oregano. Roll up chicken cigar-fashion and thread on metal or soaked bamboo skewers. Mix together oil, lemon juice, garlic, salt and pepper and brush over each roll. Place skewers on a rack on a broiling pan and broil for about 3 to 4 minutes per side, or until cooked through.

THAI CHICKEN KEBABS

Lemon grass lends an intriguing citrus-ginger tang to these neat kebabs. This herb is available fresh in Oriental markets and is easy to grow in mild climates. A big patch thrives in my Northern California garden.

4 boneless, skinless chicken breast halves
1/3 cup dry white wine
2 tbs. soy sauce
1 1/2 tbs. lemon juice
1 clove garlic, minced
1 tsp. minced fresh ginger
2 tsp. minced lemon grass or grated fresh
    lemon peel (zest)
1 tsp. freshly ground coriander seeds
Peanut Sauce, follows

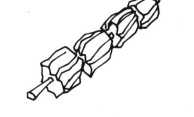

Cut chicken into 1-inch cubes. In a bowl, combine wine, soy sauce, lemon juice, garlic, ginger, lemon grass and coriander. Add chicken, cover and refrigerate for 2 hours.

Prepare a hot barbecue fire or heat grill or broiler to high. Bring chicken to room temperature before cooking. Thread chicken on metal or soaked bamboo skewers. Brush with marinade. Grill or broil for about 8 to 10 minutes, turning, or until cooked through. Serve with *Peanut Sauce*.

PEANUT SAUCE

1/4 tsp. ground cumin
1/4 tsp. ground coriander
1/4 tsp. ground turmeric
1/4 tsp. ground pepper
1 tsp. sesame oil
1 shallot, chopped

2 tbs. creamy peanut butter
1 tsp. lemon juice
2 tbs. ketchup
1/2 tsp. brown sugar
dash hot pepper sauce

In a small saucepan, sauté cumin, coriander, turmeric and pepper in sesame oil for 1 minute. Add shallot, peanut butter, lemon juice, ketchup, brown sugar and hot sauce. Stir to blend.

CHICKEN AND PEPPER KEBABS MOROCCAN

Servings: 4

Colorful skewers of chicken and peppers make an eye-catching plate when drizzled with red pepper sauce.

2 tsp. curry powder
1/4 tsp. ground cloves
1/4 tsp. ground allspice
2 tbs. lemon juice
1/4 cup plain yogurt
2 tsp. sesame oil
4 boneless, skinless chicken breast halves,
   cut into 1-inch cubes
8 pearl onions, peeled and boiled for 5 minutes
1 red bell pepper, halved, seeded and cut into 1-inch pieces
1 green or gold bell pepper, halved, seeded and cut into 1-inch pieces
Roasted Red Pepper Sauce, follows

In a bowl, stir together curry powder, cloves, allspice, lemon juice, yogurt and sesame oil. Add chicken, cover and refrigerate for 1 hour or longer.

Prepare a hot barbecue fire or heat grill or broiler to high. Thread chicken cubes and vegetables on metal or soaked bamboo skewers, starting and ending with an onion and alternating pepper chunks between. Grill or broil for about 8 to 10 minutes, turning, or until cooked through. Baste once or twice while cooking with remaining marinade. Serve with *Roasted Red Pepper Sauce.*

ROASTED RED PEPPER SAUCE

1 red bell pepper
1 tsp. olive oil
1/2 cup diced onion
1/2 tsp. chili powder

1 tbs. tomato paste
1/3 cup chicken stock, plus more if
   needed
1 tbs. balsamic or sherry vinegar

Heat broiler. Cut red pepper in half and remove seeds; flatten pepper halves with the palm of your hand. Place pepper on a broiling pan skin-side up and broil until the skin is charred. Immediately plunge charred pepper into a bowl of ice water. When cool, drain, and peel and discard skin. In a skillet, heat olive oil over medium heat and sauté onion and chili powder for 3 to 4 minutes; add tomato paste and cook for 3 minutes longer, stirring once or twice. In a blender container, place pepper, onion mixture, chicken stock and vinegar and process until blended. If necessary, add additional stock to make desired consistency. Return sauce to skillet and heat through.

INDONESIAN CHICKEN SATÉ

This typical Indonesian dish packs a lively flavor due to the intriguing medley of spices in the sauce. If you use bamboo skewers, soak them in warm water for 20 minutes before using, which prevents them from burning.

4 boneless, skinless chicken breast halves
1 medium onion, chopped
4 tsp. freshly ground coriander seeds
dash cayenne pepper
1½ tbs. brown sugar
2 cloves garlic, minced
salt and freshly ground black pepper to taste
3 tbs. lemon juice
¼ cup soy sauce
Saté Sauce, follows

Cut chicken into 1-inch cubes. In a medium bowl, place onion, coriander, cayenne, sugar, garlic, salt, pepper, lemon juice and soy sauce and mix well. Add chicken, stir to coat, cover and refrigerate for 2 hours or longer.

Prepare a hot barbecue fire or heat grill or broiler to high. Thread chicken on metal or soaked bamboo skewers and grill or broil for about 8 to 10 minutes, turning, until cooked through. Serve with *Saté Sauce*.

SATÉ SAUCE

1/4 tsp. ground cumin
1/4 tsp. ground coriander
1/4 tsp. ground turmeric
1/4 tsp. ground pepper
1/2 tsp. olive oil
2 tbs. creamy peanut butter
1 tsp. lemon juice

1/4 cup water
1/2 tsp. brown sugar
1 clove garlic, minced
1 tbs. chopped shallot or green onion
    white part only
salt to taste
hot pepper sauce to taste

In a small skillet over medium heat, sauté cumin, coriander, turmeric and pepper in olive oil for 1 to 2 minutes. Add peanut butter, lemon juice, water, brown sugar, garlic and chopped shallot. Season with salt and hot pepper sauce.

CHICKEN BROCHETTES ALEXANDRIA

Servings: 4

For a sophisticated take on Egyptian dining, I like to serve these spicy kebabs of golden chicken and red peppers with grilled slices of sesame oil-basted eggplant.

½ tsp. olive oil
1 tbs. curry powder
½ tsp. ground turmeric
½ tsp. ground cardamom
½ tsp. ground allspice
2 tbs. plain yogurt
1 tbs. tahini (sesame seed paste)
1 tbs. lemon juice
1 tbs. cider vinegar
salt and freshly ground pepper to taste

4 boneless, skinless chicken breast
    halves, cut into 1-inch pieces
8 cherry tomatoes
8 small boiling onions, peeled and
    boiled for 5 minutes
1 small red bell pepper, seeded and cut
    into 1-inch pieces
plain yogurt, optional
chopped chives, optional

In a small skillet over medium heat, heat oil and sauté spices for 2 to 3 minutes. In a large bowl, mix yogurt, tahini, lemon juice, vinegar, spice mixture, salt and pepper. Add chicken and marinate for 30 minutes. Prepare a hot barbecue fire or heat grill or broiler to high. Thread chicken on metal or soaked bamboo skewers, alternating with tomatoes, onions and pepper. Grill or broil for about 8 to 10 minutes, turning, until cooked through. If desired, pass yogurt seasoned with chopped chives for a sauce.

CHICKEN TANDOORI

Couscous or saffron rice and grilled eggplant topped with a fresh ginger-spiked tomato sauce make superb accompaniments to these spicy chicken breasts.

1/4 tsp. saffron threads
2 tbs. hot water
1 1/2 tbs. coriander seeds
1 tsp. cumin seeds
3 whole cloves
seeds from 4 cardamom pods
small piece dried red chile pepper, such as ancho or chipotle

3/4 cup plain yogurt
1/2 medium onion, quartered
1 tbs. chopped fresh ginger
1 large clove garlic, minced
4 boneless, skinless chicken breast halves
lemon or lime wedges for garnish

Soak saffron in hot water for a few minutes. In a small skillet over low heat, toast coriander and cumin seeds, cloves, cardamom and chile for 3 to 4 minutes, stirring or shaking pan frequently. Place yogurt, onion, ginger and garlic in a blender container or food processor workbowl and blend until smooth. Add roasted seed mixture and saffron with liquid and blend until smooth. Place chicken pieces in a bowl and pour marinade over. Cover and refrigerate for at least 2 hours or overnight.

Prepare a hot barbecue fire or heat grill or broiler to high. Grill or broil chicken for about 8 to 10 minutes, turning, until cooked through. Garnish with lemon wedges.

FAJITAS

These "wraps" are easily made in quantity for a crowd. I like to serve them with black beans as a side dish, a fruit platter of melon and grapes as an accompaniment and homemade mango sorbet or root beer floats for dessert.

4 boneless, skinless chicken breast halves
1 tbs. olive oil
2 cloves garlic, minced
1 shallot or green onion, white part only, chopped
¼ cup dry white wine
4 large flour or whole wheat tortillas
1 small avocado, peeled and sliced, optional
Cilantro-Sesame Sauce, follows

Place chicken in a locking plastic bag with oil, garlic, shallot or green onion and wine. Seal bag and refrigerate for 1 hour.

Prepare a hot barbecue fire or heat grill or broiler to high. Remove chicken from marinade and grill or broil for about 8 to 10 minutes, turning, until cooked through.

Wrap tortillas in aluminum foil and warm on the grill or in a 350° oven for about 10 minutes. Slice chicken thinly on the diagonal, distribute on warm tortillas and top with avocado slices, if using, and *Cilantro-Sesame Sauce*.

CILANTRO-SESAME SAUCE

¾ cup chopped red onion
salt
½ cup chopped fresh cilantro
1 tbs. sesame oil

Sprinkle onion lightly with salt and let stand for 10 minutes, until liquid is released; rinse well under cold running water and pat dry. Place onion in a small bowl and stir in chopped cilantro and sesame oil.

CHICKEN BREASTS WITH MANGO SALSA

Servings: 4

A ginger and lime-zested fruit salsa lends a vibrant tang to grilled chicken.

RASPBERRY-LIME MARINADE

2 tbs. raspberry vinegar
2 tbs. lime juice
1 tbs. Dijon mustard
1 tbs. chopped fresh tarragon, or ¾ tsp. dried
1 tbs. chopped fresh thyme, or ¾ tsp. dried
1 tbs. olive oil

MANGO SALSA

2 cups diced fresh mango
½ cup diced red onion
½ cup halved cherry tomatoes or diced red bell pepper
¼ cup chopped fresh cilantro or flat-leaf parsley
2 tbs. lime juice
2 tsp. minced fresh ginger

4 boneless, skinless chicken breast halves
chopped fresh cilantro or flat-leaf parsley for garnish

Stir together marinade ingredients and set aside. Stir together salsa ingredients and set aside.

Place chicken breasts in a locking plastic bag and add *Raspberry-Lime Marinade*. Seal bag and let stand at room temperature for 30 minutes. Prepare a hot barbecue fire or heat grill or broiler to high. Grill or broil chicken for about 8 to 10 minutes, turning once, or until cooked through. Arrange on a serving dish and spoon *Mango Salsa* alongside. Garnish with cilantro or parsley.

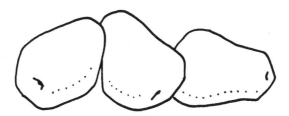

GRILLED CHICKEN SANTA FE

Bold and colorful Southwestern ingredients characterize this festive entrée. Soft polenta or black beans make a delightful accompaniment along with a pitcher of sangria. Use your own own homemade salsa or taco sauce or buy a commercially prepared one.

4 boneless, skinless chicken breast
   halves
1 tsp. chili powder
1 tsp. ground cumin
½ tsp. dried oregano
salt and freshly ground pepper to taste
shredded iceberg lettuce

chile salsa or taco sauce
1 large ripe avocado
plain yogurt for garnish
12 cherry tomatoes, halved, for garnish
3 green onions, with half of the green
   tops, chopped, for garnish

Prepare a hot barbecue fire or heat grill or broiler to high. Rub chicken with chili powder, cumin, oregano, salt and pepper. Grill or broil chicken for about 8 to 10 minutes, turning, or until cooked through.

On a platter, arrange a bed of shredded lettuce and drizzle with salsa. Top with grilled chicken, sliced and fanned, if desired. Peel and slice avocado and arrange in pinwheels alongside chicken. Dollop with yogurt and scatter cherry tomatoes and green onions over all.

GRILLED CHICKEN AND RED PEPPERS

A red pepper sauce coats grilled chicken and red peppers for a Southwest-inspired entrée. Accompany with black beans and a green salad embellished with pink grapefruit segments and avocado slices. See page 107 for instructions on washing fermented black beans.

3 tbs. olive oil
1/4 cup fresh lemon or grapefruit juice
3 tbs. washed fermented black beans
1 bunch fresh cilantro, chopped
4 chicken breast halves, or 8 chicken
    thighs, or 1 broiler-fryer, quartered

1 tbs. olive oil
1 tbs. lemon juice
2 red bell peppers, quartered length-
    wise and seeded
fresh cilantro sprigs for garnish

In a large locking plastic bag, mix 3 tbs. oil, 1/4 cup lemon juice, black beans and chopped cilantro. Add chicken and turn to coat all sides with marinade. Seal bag and refrigerate for at least 2 hours.

Prepare a hot barbecue fire or heat grill or broiler to high. Mix 1 tbs. olive oil and 1 tbs. lemon juice and brush over peppers. Remove chicken from marinade. Grill or broil peppers and chicken, turning, for about 12 to 15 minutes for peppers and breasts, and 20 to 25 minutes for thighs or quarters, or until cooked through. Arrange on warm serving plates and garnish with cilantro.

CHICKEN PATTIES WITH SUN-DRIED TOMATOES

Servings: 2

A flavorful topping of Jarlsberg cheese and sun-dried tomatoes elevates broiled ground chicken patties. Accompany with a spinach, pear and toasted hazelnut salad. Chocolate or strawberry frozen yogurt sundaes make a fast dessert.

½ lb. ground chicken
¼ cup fine dry breadcrumbs
1 tbs. dry sherry
1 tbs. balsamic vinegar
1 clove garlic, minced
1 tsp. chopped fresh oregano or thyme, or ¼ tsp. dried

2 tbs. chopped fresh flat-leaf parsley
¼ tsp. ground allspice
salt and freshly ground pepper to taste
1½ tbs. stone-ground mustard
1 oz. Jarlsberg cheese, sliced
4 oil-packed sun-dried tomatoes

Heat broiler. Mix chicken with breadcrumbs, sherry, vinegar, garlic, oregano, parsley, allspice, salt and pepper. Shape into 2 patties about ½-inch thick. Place patties on a broiling pan and broil for about 3 to 4 minutes per side, or until cooked through. Spread with mustard, top with cheese and tomatoes, and return to broiler just until cheese melts.

BARBECUED CHICKEN

This lively tomato-based barbecue sauce gilds chicken with a wonderful old-fashioned traditional flavor.

1 can (8 oz.) tomato sauce
¼ cup cider vinegar
1 tbs. sugar
1 tbs. molasses
2 cloves garlic, minced

¼ cup chopped onion
1 tsp. dry mustard
salt and cayenne pepper to taste
two broiler-fryers, about 3-3½ lb. each,
    quartered

Prepare a hot barbecue fire. In a saucepan, combine tomato sauce, vinegar, sugar, molasses, garlic, onion, mustard, salt and cayenne. Bring to a boil; reduce heat to low and simmer for 3 minutes, stirring constantly. Grill chicken quarters over hot coals, basting with sauce during the last 5 to 8 minutes of cooking and turning chicken pieces every 10 minutes. Cook for about 30 to 35 minutes, or until cooked through.

NOTE: Breasts may be done 5 to 10 minutes before other parts.

ROASTS AND BAKES

SUPREME ROASTED CHICKEN WITH HERBS

A high oven temperature produces the ultimate roasted chicken with a wonderful crisp crust and moist white and dark meat. If you have time, plan to refrigerate the chicken overnight for the seasonings to thoroughly permeate it. After roasting, the chicken is so flavorful and juicy it doesn't need a sauce.

1 broiler-fryer, about 3-3½ lb.
sea salt and freshly ground pepper to taste
juice of ½ lemon
12 fresh sage or lemon balm leaves, or
    more to taste

8 cloves garlic, minced
1 lb. small new potatoes, such as red
    creamer or Yukon gold, optional
2 tbs. olive oil

Remove innards and any excessive fat from chicken. Season with salt and pepper, sprinkle with lemon juice and stuff sage or lemon balm leaves under the skin of breast and thighs. Scatter some of the garlic inside chicken cavity and stuff remaining garlic under breast skin. Place chicken breast-side down on a rack in a large roasting pan. Set aside at room temperature for 30 minutes.

Heat oven to 450°. Roast chicken for 20 minutes. Turn chicken breast-side up and roast for 30 to 40 minutes, or until done (see page 8). If desired, toss potatoes in oil and place in pan during the last 20 to 25 minutes of roasting, until cooked through. If pan juices are browning too fast, add a little water to roasting pan.

ROASTED CHICKEN WITH ROASTED VEGETABLES

By synchronizing the timing, roasting assorted new potatoes, summer squash and red onion slices along with the bird makes for an easy-to-achieve dinner, all on one platter.

1 broiler-fryer, about 3-3½ lb.
salt and freshly ground pepper to taste
1 tbs. chopped fresh oregano, or ¾ tsp. dried
4 slices lemon
1 carrot, cut into 1-inch chunks
1 tsp. olive oil
¼ cup water
12 small new red, Yukon gold and/or blue potatoes, halved

2 zucchini or yellow summer squash, cut into ½-inch-thick diagonal slices
1 large red onion, cut into ⅜-inch-thick slices
1 tbs. extra virgin olive oil
1 tbs. balsamic vinegar
2 tsp. Dijon mustard
2 large cloves garlic, minced
¼ cup dry vermouth
¼ cup chicken stock

Heat oven to 450°. Remove innards and any excessive fat from chicken and season with salt and pepper. Sprinkle oregano inside chicken cavity and add lemon slices. Toss carrot with 1 tsp. oil and water and place in the bottom of a roasting pan. Place chicken breast-side down on a rack in roasting pan. Roast for 20 minutes. Toss potatoes, zucchini and onion in 1 tbs. oil, vinegar, mustard and garlic and place on a greased baking sheet. Turn chicken breast-side up and roast chicken and vegetables for 40 to 45 minutes, basting chicken with vermouth and roasting until vegetables are tender and chicken is done (see page 8). Pour off pan juices from roasted chicken into a saucepan, skim fat from the surface and discard carrot; add stock and bring to a boil, stirring. Carve chicken into serving pieces and serve with potatoes and onions. Pass pan juices.

ROASTED CHICKEN WITH MUSHROOMS AND CREAM

In this glorious French-style recipe, cream coats a large plump bird with a mahogany glaze and mingles with the pan juices to form a rich mushroom sauce.

1 roaster, about 4-4½ lb.
2 tbs. chopped fresh tarragon
1 shallot, minced
1 tbs. butter, room temperature
salt and freshly ground pepper to taste
1 lemon or orange
4 cloves garlic, minced
1 cup heavy cream
2 tbs. cognac or brandy
½ lb. small white mushrooms, halved if desired
3 tbs. chopped fresh chives for garnish

Remove innards and any excessive fat from chicken. Blend tarragon and shallot with butter and rub under chicken breast skin. Place chicken on a rack breast-side down in a roasting pan and season with salt and pepper. Quarter lemon or orange and place inside chicken cavity with ½ of the garlic. Scatter remaining garlic outside chicken. Let stand at room temperature for 30 minutes.

Heat oven to 425°. Roast chicken for 20 minutes. Turn chicken breast-side up and reduce oven heat to 375°. Pour ½ of the cream blended with cognac over chicken and roast for 30 minutes. Pour over remaining cream and place mushrooms in pan juices. Roast for 30 to 40 minutes longer, or until done (see page 8), basting several times with juices. Skim fat from the surface of sauce. Carve chicken into serving pieces and serve with mushroom sauce, garnished with chopped chives.

ROASTED CHICKEN ORANGERIE

A zestful orange and glazed onion sauce gilds chicken for a party dish.

1 broiler-fryer, about 3-3½ lb.
2 cloves garlic, minced
1 tbs. chopped fresh tarragon, or ¾ tsp. dried
salt and freshly ground pepper to taste
2 navel oranges
½ cup chicken stock
16 small boiling onions, peeled
1 tsp. butter or olive oil
3 tbs. frozen orange juice concentrate, thawed
arugula leaves for garnish

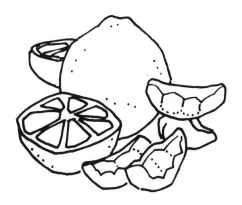

Remove innards and any excessive fat from chicken. Place garlic and tarragon under chicken breast skin and season chicken with salt and pepper. Place chicken breast-side down on a rack in a roasting pan. With a vegetable peeler, remove several strips of orange peel (zest) and place inside chicken cavity. Let stand at room temperature for 30 minutes.

Heat oven to 425°. Roast chicken for 20 minutes; reduce oven heat to 375°, turn chicken breast-side up and roast for 50 minutes, or until done (see page 8), adding a little water to pan drippings if necessary to keep from browning too much. Place chicken on a platter, cover with aluminum foil and keep warm.

Pour off pan juices and skim fat from the surface. Pour chicken stock into pan and scrape up browned bits. In a medium saucepan, sauté onions in butter or oil until soft. Add chicken stock and drippings, cover and simmer for 10 minutes, or until onions are tender. Stir in orange juice concentrate and heat until blended. Carve chicken into serving pieces and spoon onions and sauce over chicken. Peel and slice oranges and arrange a few slices alongside each serving. Garnish with arugula.

ROASTED CHICKEN WITH GRAPES

Grapes burst with juiciness after roasting inside a bird for an easy-to-execute dish. This has lots of flair with minimal effort.

1 broiler-fryer, about 3-3½ lb.
2 tbs. lemon juice
salt, pepper and paprika to taste
1½ cups seedless green or red grapes
2 tsp. grated fresh lemon peel (zest)

1 large onion, cut into ½-inch-thick
  slices
2 tsp. olive oil
¼ cup water
⅓ cup dry white wine

Remove innards and any excessive fat from chicken. Drizzle chicken with lemon juice and sprinkle with salt, pepper and paprika. In a bowl, toss grapes with lemon peel and place inside chicken cavity. In a bowl, toss onion with oil and water and place in the bottom of a roasting pan. Place chicken breast-side down on a rack in roasting pan and let stand at room temperature for 30 minutes.

Heat oven to 450°. Roast chicken for 20 minutes; turn chicken breast-side up and roast for about 40 minutes, or until done (see page 8), basting several times with wine and drippings. Transfer chicken and onions to a warm platter. Skim fat from the surface of pan juices. Carve chicken into serving pieces and serve grapes alongside. Pass pan juices.

ORIENTAL ROASTED CHICKEN

Oriental seasonings — soy sauce, sesame seeds and ginger — flavor this easy roasted chicken dish, ideal for all seasons. The spicy chicken is good hot or cold, so consider it for picnic or patio fare as well as cool weather dining.

1 broiler-fryer, about 3-3½ lb.
2 shallots or green onions, white part only, minced
3 cloves garlic, minced
1 tbs. chopped fresh ginger
¼ cup light soy sauce
2 tbs. dry sherry
1 tsp. honey

Remove innards and any excessive fat from chicken . Place ½ of the shallots and garlic in chicken cavity. In a large bowl, mix remaining shallots and garlic with ginger, soy sauce, sherry and honey. Add chicken and marinate, turning occasionally, for 1 hour.

Heat oven to 425°. Place chicken on a rack in a roasting pan breast-side down and roast for 20 minutes. Reduce oven heat to 375°, turn chicken breast-side up and roast for 50 to 60 minutes, or until done (see page 8), basting occasionally with marinade. Carve chicken into serving pieces.

ROASTED CHICKEN WITH ROSEMARY AND GARLIC NUGGETS

Servings: 4-6

A golden bird makes a festive entrée for family dining with children of all ages. If desired, roast 2 broiler-fryers and use the leftover chicken for salad, pitas or fajitas.

1 broiler-fryer, about 3-3½ lb.
salt and freshly ground pepper to taste
2 tbs. chopped fresh rosemary or tarragon, or 1½ tsp. dried
½ cup dry white vermouth or wine
2 large heads garlic
1 tsp. butter or olive oil
rosemary or tarragon sprigs for garnish

Remove innards and any excessive fat from chicken; season chicken with salt and pepper and sprinkle rosemary or tarragon inside chicken cavity. Place chicken breast-side down on a rack in a roasting pan. Let stand at room temperature for 30 minutes.

Heat oven to 450°. Roast chicken for 20 minutes. Turn chicken breast-side up and roast for 40 minutes, basting with vermouth, until done (see page 8).

While chicken is roasting, separate garlic head into cloves, but do not peel. Place cloves in a small saucepan and cover with water. Bring to a boil, reduce heat to low and simmer for 5 minutes; drain completely and repeat process twice; drain thoroughly. Cool garlic cloves and remove skins. Sauté garlic cloves in butter or oil for 2 to 3 minutes, or until barely browned. Pour off pan juices from roasted chicken and skim fat from the surface. Carve chicken into serving pieces and scatter several garlic cloves over each serving. Garnish with rosemary sprigs and pass pan juices.

ROASTED CHICKEN WITH APPLES, YAMS AND ONIONS

Caramelized onions, yams and apples accompany this savory autumn entrée.

1 broiler-fryer, about 3-3½ lb.
salt and freshly ground pepper to taste
2 large cloves garlic, minced
12 fresh sage leaves, or ¾ tsp. dried
1 large onion, cut into ⅜-inch-thick slices
4 tsp. olive oil

¼ cup water
3 medium yams, peeled and cut into
　⅜-inch-thick slices
2 Granny Smith apples, quartered, cored
¼ cup fruity white wine, such as Chenin
　Blanc or Johannisberg Riesling

Remove innards and any excessive fat from chicken. Season chicken with salt and pepper and place garlic and sage under chicken breast skin and inside cavity. Toss onion in 1 tsp. of the oil and water and place in a roasting pan. Place chicken breast-side down on a rack in roasting pan. Let stand at room temperature for 30 minutes.

Heat oven to 450°. Roast chicken for 20 minutes. Toss yams and apples in remaining oil and place around chicken. Turn chicken breast-side up and roast for 40 to 45 minutes, basting with wine, until yams are tender and chicken is done (see page 8). Pour off pan juices and skim fat from the surface. Carve chicken into serving pieces and serve with yams, apples and onions. Pass pan juices.

MUSTARD- AND HERB-GLAZED CHICKEN BREASTS

A tangy lemon, mustard and fresh herb coating enhances chicken breasts for a succulent finish. Serve with wedges of polenta topped with sun-dried tomatoes, steamed sugar snap peas and fresh spinach tossed with balsamic vinaigrette and toasted pine nuts.

4 boneless, skinless chicken breast
   halves
1 lemon
1/4 cup mixed minced fresh rosemary,
   oregano, flat-leaf parsley and
   tarragon, or 3/4 tbs. mixed dried herbs

2 tbs. Dijon mustard
2 tbs. dry white wine
2 tbs. olive oil
salt and freshly ground pepper to taste
2 cloves garlic, minced
lemon wedges for garnish

Place chicken in a baking dish. Remove lemon peel (zest) with a citrus zester or vegetable peeler; cut into very thin strips if needed. Juice lemon. Combine lemon peel and juice with herbs, mustard, wine, oil, salt, pepper and garlic and spread over chicken. Cover and refrigerate for 2 hours or longer.

Heat oven to 375° and bake chicken for 15 minutes, or until cooked through. Serve garnished with lemon wedges.

CHICKEN BREASTS STUFFED WITH SUN-DRIED TOMATO PESTO

Slip a stuffing of tomato pesto under the skin of chicken for an aromatic, succulent entrée. Other pestos, such as olive or basil blended with ricotta cheese, work well, too.

SUN-DRIED TOMATO PESTO
1 cup dry sun-dried tomatoes
1/3 cup water
4 cloves garlic, minced
1/3 cup fresh flat-leaf parsley sprigs, packed
2 tbs. chopped fresh garlic chives or green onion tops
2 tbs. pistachio nuts or pine nuts
2 tbs. olive oil
2 tbs. freshly grated Parmesan or Romano cheese

6 boneless chicken breast halves, skin attached
salt and freshly ground pepper to taste
about 1 bunch arugula or fresh basil

For pesto, simmer tomatoes in water for 3 minutes; cool to room temperature. Place tomatoes, garlic, parsley, garlic chives and nuts in a food processor workbowl. Process until finely minced. Add oil and cheese and process until well mixed.

Heat oven to 400°. Rub about 2 tbs. of the pesto under skin of each chicken breast. Place in a baking pan, tucking the long ends underneath to form plump mounds, and season with salt and pepper. Bake for 20 to 25 minutes, or until cooked through. Cut in half diagonally and serve on a bed of arugula or basil.

CHUTNEY-GLAZED CHICKEN BREASTS

Servings: 2

This easy chicken entrée acquires an appealing mahogany glaze from its mustard and apricot chutney coating. Accompany with white and wild rice or couscous. For an attractive presentation, line a small custard cup with plastic wrap, spoon in the rice or couscous, pat down and invert onto a plate. Repeat with remaining servings and arrange chicken alongside.

2 tsp. sweet-hot mustard
2 tbs. apricot or mango chutney
2 tsp. soy sauce
2 boneless, skinless chicken breast halves
salt and freshly ground pepper to taste
1 orange, peeled and sliced, for garnish
watercress or arugula leaves for garnish

Heat oven to 400°. Mix mustard, chutney and soy sauce and use to coat chicken. Season with salt and pepper. Place in an oiled baking pan. Bake for 12 to 15 minutes, or until cooked through. Serve garnished with orange slices and watercress or arugula.

CHICKEN AND FENNEL IN PARCHMENT PACKETS

For an entrée surprise, parchment encases chicken breasts on a bed of vegetables, accented with the licorice bite of fresh fennel.

2 tbs. olive oil
2 boneless, skinless chicken breast
   halves
2 tsp. Dijon mustard
1 stalk fennel, cut into fine matchstick
   strips
1 small carrot, cut into fine matchstick
   strips

1 shallot, cut into fine matchstick
   strips
1 tbs. chopped fresh flat-leaf parsley
1 tsp. chopped fresh thyme, or ¼ tsp.
   dried
salt and freshly ground pepper to taste

Heat oven to 375°. Fold two 10-x-15-inch pieces of parchment paper in half crosswise; trim corners to form ovals. Open ovals and brush with ½ of the oil, leaving a 1-inch border. Place 1 chicken breast in the center of each oval; spread with mustard and sprinkle with fennel, carrot, shallot, parsley, thyme, salt and pepper. Drizzle with remaining oil. Fold paper over chicken and crimp the edges to seal. Place on a baking sheet and bake for 15 to 20 minutes, or until chicken is cooked through. Serve on dinner plates.

CHICKEN IN PARCHMENT
WITH EGGPLANT AND ZUCCHINI

Servings: 2

These neat dinner packets encase chicken thighs and ratatouille to eat with a dollop of pesto.

2 tbs. olive oil
2 large chicken thighs
2 tsp. stone-ground mustard
1 small Japanese eggplant, diced
1 small zucchini, diced
1 small red onion, sliced and separated
   into rings

6 cherry tomatoes, halved
1 tbs. chopped fresh flat-leaf parsley
1 tsp. chopped fresh oregano, or
   1/4 tsp. dried
salt and freshly ground pepper to taste
pesto

Heat oven to 375°. Fold two 10-x-15-inch pieces of parchment paper in half crosswise; trim corners to form ovals. Open ovals and brush with half of the oil, leaving a 1-inch border. Place 1 chicken thigh in the center of each oval; spread with mustard. Toss eggplant, zucchini, onion, tomatoes, parsley and oregano with remaining oil and spread over chicken; sprinkle with salt and pepper. Fold paper over chicken and crimp the edges to seal. Bake for 35 minutes, or until chicken is cooked through. Serve on dinner plates and pass pesto.

CHICKEN AND SPUDS IN A BAG

For an amusing presentation, dinner bakes in a paper lunch bag and goes to the table enclosed, letting the wonderful aromas explode as the bag is opened.

2 lunch-sized brown or white paper bags
olive oil
4 small Yukon gold or red creamer
potatoes, peeled and cut into 3/8-inch-
thick slices
1 small zucchini, cut into 3/8-inch-thick
slices
1 small yellow crookneck squash, cut
into 3/8-inch-thick slices

4 chicken thighs
salt and freshly ground pepper to taste
1 clove garlic, minced
1 shallot, chopped
2 tsp. minced fresh oregano
2 tsp. minced fresh flat-leaf parsley
1 tbs. olive oil

Heat oven to 375°. Lightly oil the inside bottom of paper bags and place on a baking pan. Toss potatoes, zucchini, squash and chicken with salt, pepper, garlic, shallots, herbs and olive oil. Distribute vegetables evenly in bags and place chicken on top of vegetables. Fold down tops of bags and secure with 2 paper clips each. Bake for 30 to 35 minutes, or until potatoes and chicken are cooked through. Serve on dinner plates.

CHICKEN AND LEEK STRUDELS

These plump filo pastries make a delectable entrée for a luncheon or a buffet party. The tissue-thin pastry can dry out swiftly and become as fragile as onion skin. Keep it covered with plastic wrap or a towel while working with it. If you buy filo frozen, let it first thaw overnight in the refrigerator before using.

1 barbecued or roasted broiler-fryer, about 3-3½ lb.
4 tbs. butter
1 bunch leeks, white part only, chopped
1 carrot, shredded
¼ cup chopped fresh flat-leaf parsley
¾ tsp. dried tarragon, crumbled
salt and freshly ground pepper to taste
2 eggs, beaten
1½ cups (6 oz.) shredded Jarlsberg or Gruyère cheese
6 sheets filo dough

Heat oven to 375°. Remove and discard skin and bones from chicken and cut meat into bite-sized pieces (you should have about 4 cups). Place chicken in a bowl. In a skillet, melt 1 tbs. of the butter and sauté leeks and carrot until soft. Add to chicken along with parsley, tarragon, salt, pepper, eggs and cheese and mix lightly.

Melt remaining butter in a small saucepan. Lay filo on a work surface and cover with plastic wrap. Using 1 sheet at a time, brush filo lightly with melted butter and fold sheet in half, making a 9-x-12-inch rectangle; brush again with butter. Spoon about ⅔ cup of the chicken filling in a strip along one of the short ends. Fold in the long sides about 1¼ inches and roll up, making a roll about 6½ inches long and 1½ inches wide. Place roll seam-side down on a lightly greased baking sheet. Repeat process with remaining filling and filo. Brush the tops of rolls with butter. Bake rolls for 20 to 25 minutes, or until golden brown.

CHICKEN AND MUSHROOM FILO ROLLS

Servings: 8

You can barbecue or roast an extra broiler-fryer one night to make these mushroom- and cheese-enriched filo pastries the next day. Or, pick up a roasted chicken at the deli.

1 tbs. olive oil
1 medium white onion, chopped
3 green onions, with half of the green tops, chopped
4 tbs. butter
½ lb. white mushrooms, finely chopped
2 cloves garlic, minced
1 barbecued or roasted broiler-fryer, about 3-3½ lb.
¼ cup chopped fresh flat-leaf parsley
dash nutmeg
3 eggs
2 cups (8 oz.) shredded Gruyère or Emmentaler cheese
8 sheets filo dough

Heat oven to 375°. In a large skillet over medium-high heat, heat oil and sauté white and green onions in oil for about 5 minutes, until softened. Add 1 tbs. of the butter, mushrooms and garlic and cook for about 2 minutes, until just softened. Remove and discard skin and bones from chicken and cut meat into bite-sized pieces (you should have about 4 cups). Place chicken in a bowl and add sautéed vegetables, parsley, nutmeg, eggs and cheese; mix well.

Melt remaining butter in a small saucepan. Lay filo on a work surface and cover with plastic wrap. Using 1 sheet at a time, brush filo lightly with melted butter and fold sheet in half, making a 9-x-12-inch rectangle; brush again with butter. Spoon about ⅔ cup of the chicken filling in a strip along one of the short ends. Fold in the long sides about 1¼ inches and roll up, making a roll about 6½ inches long and 1½ inches wide. Place roll seam-side down on a lightly greased baking sheet. Repeat process with remaining filling and filo. Brush the tops of rolls with butter. Bake rolls for 20 to 25 minutes, or until golden brown.

WINE-GLAZED CHICKEN DRUMSTICKS

Servings: 4

Herb-seasoned chicken drumsticks are excellent hot or cold for picnic fare. This is a great make-ahead dish, as it reheats nicely to serve with polenta or couscous, or it can be cooked in the cool of the day for a summer outing.

8 chicken drumsticks or thighs
peel (zest) of 1 lemon, slivered
1½ tbs. lemon juice
½ cup dry red wine
1 tbs. olive oil
1 tbs. chopped fresh rosemary, or
   ¾ tsp. dried

2 tbs. chopped fresh flat-leaf parsley
1 shallot or green onion, white part
   only, chopped
1 clove garlic, minced
salt and freshly ground pepper to taste
1 lemon, thinly sliced and seeded

In a bowl, mix together lemon peel, lemon juice, wine, oil, rosemary, parsley, shallot, garlic, salt and pepper. Place chicken in a locking plastic bag, add marinade, seal and refrigerate for 2 hours or longer.

Heat oven to 425°. Place chicken in a baking dish and add lemon slices. Pour over half of the marinade. Bake chicken for 30 to 35 minutes, or until cooked through, basting with remaining marinade. If necessary, add a little water to pan to keep it from drying out.

FIVE-SPICE CHICKEN LEGS

The exotic overtones of Chinese five-spice powder permeate chicken legs for this taste-tingling entrée. Cinnamon, star anise and cloves dominate this sultry spice blend, which is available in powder form in Asian markets or good supermarkets. For an East-West menu, accompany with roasted yams, and red onion and napa cabbage slaw; savor candied ginger ice cream and sesame cookies for dessert.

4 chicken legs, thighs attached
salt and freshly ground pepper to taste
1 tsp. Chinese five-spice powder
2 tbs. soy sauce

2 tbs. dry sherry
1 tsp. chopped fresh ginger
1 clove garlic, minced
2 tsp. sesame oil

Heat oven to 425°. Rub chicken pieces with salt, pepper and five-spice powder and place on a rack in a baking pan. Bake for 20 minutes. In a bowl, mix together soy sauce, sherry, ginger, garlic and sesame oil and brush half of it over chicken. Bake for 20 more minutes, or until cooked through, basting with remaining sauce.

CHICKEN AND MANGOES PACIFIC-STYLE

Servings: 2-3

The lively seasonings of chutney, sesame oil and ginger lend verve to dark-meated chicken thighs, partnered with a refreshing accent of fruit. Seedless grapes can stand in for the mango, papaya or tangerine segments.

3 tbs. mango or apricot chutney
2 tbs. lime juice
1 tsp. soy sauce
1 tsp. sesame oil
1 clove garlic, minced
1 tsp. minced lemon grass or fresh
    lemon peel (zest)

1 tsp. minced fresh ginger
4 chicken thighs, skinned if desired
hot cooked couscous or bulgur
diced mango, diced papaya or tangerine
    segments for garnish
arugula leaves or watercress for garnish

In a large bowl, stir together chutney, lime juice, soy sauce, sesame oil, garlic, lemon grass and ginger. Place chicken in a greased baking pan and spread with chutney mixture. Marinate at room temperature for 30 minutes.

Heat oven to 375°. Roast chicken for 25 to 30 minutes, or until cooked through. Serve with couscous or bulgur and garnish with fruit and arugula or watercress.

INDEX

SERVE CREATIVE, EASY, NUTRITIOUS MEALS WITH nitty gritty® COOKBOOKS

Beer and Good Food
Unbeatable Chicken Recipes
Gourmet Gifts
From Freezer, 'Fridge and Pantry
Edible Pockets for Every Meal
Cooking With Chile Peppers
Oven and Rotisserie Roasting
Risottos, Paellas and Other Rice
   Specialties
Entrées From Your Bread Machine
Muffins, Nut Breads and More
Healthy Snacks for Kids
100 Dynamite Desserts
Recipes for Yogurt Cheese
Sautés
Cooking in Porcelain
Appetizers
Casseroles
The Toaster Oven Cookbook
Skewer Cooking on the Grill
Creative Mexican Cooking
Extra-Special Crockery Pot Recipes
Slow Cooking
Marinades
The Wok

No Salt, No Sugar, No Fat Cookbook
Quick and Easy Pasta Recipes
Cooking in Clay
Deep Fried Indulgences
Cooking with Parchment Paper
The Garlic Cookbook
From Your Ice Cream Maker
Cappuccino/Espresso: The Book of
   Beverages
The Best Pizza is made at home*
The Best Bagels are made at home*
Convection Oven Cookery
The Steamer Cookbook
The Pasta Machine Cookbook
The Versatile Rice Cooker
The Dehydrator Cookbook
The Bread Machine Cookbook
The Bread Machine Cookbook II
The Bread Machine Cookbook III
The Bread Machine Cookbook IV:
   Whole Grains and Natural Sugars
The Bread Machine Cookbook V:
   Favorite Recipes from 100 Kitchens

The Bread Machine Cookbook VI:
   Hand-Shaped Breads from the
   Dough Cycle
Worldwide Sourdoughs From Your
   Bread Machine
Recipes for the Pressure Cooker
The New Blender Book
The Sandwich Maker Cookbook
Waffles
Indoor Grilling
The Coffee Book
The Juicer Books I and II
Bread Baking (traditional)
The 9x13 Pan Cookbook
Recipes for the Loaf Pan
Low Fat American Favorites
Healthy Cooking on the Run
Favorite Seafood Recipes
New International Fondue Cookbook
Favorite Cookie Recipes
Flatbreads From Around the World
Cooking for 1 or 2
The Well Dressed Potato

For a free catalog, write or call:
Bristol Publishing Enterprises, Inc.
P.O. Box 1737, San Leandro, CA 94577
(800) 346-4889; in California, (510) 895-4461

* perfect for your bread
machine